Jesse Feiler

FileMaker® 8

@work

PROJECTS AND TECHNIQUES TO GET THE JOB DONE

SAMS

800 East 96th Street, Indianapolis, Indiana 46240

FileMaker® 8 @work: Projects and Techniques to Get the Job Done

Copyright © 2006 by Sams Publishing

International Standard Book Number: 0-672-32856-9

Library of Congress Catalog Card Number: 2005930752

Printed in the United States of America

First Printing: February 2006

09   08   07   06   4   3   2   1

Trademarks

All terms mentioned in this book that are known to be trademarks or service marks have been appropriately capitalized. Sams Publishing cannot attest to the accuracy of this information. Use of a term in this book should not be regarded as affecting the validity of any trademark or service mark.

Warning and Disclaimer

Bulk Sales

Sams Publishing offers excellent discounts on this book when ordered in quantity for bulk purchases or special sales. For more information, please contact

U.S. Corporate and Government Sales
1-800-382-3419
corpsales@pearsontechgroup.com

For sales outside of the U.S., please contact

International Sales
international@pearsoned.com

Acquisitions Editor
Betsy Brown

Development Editor
Scott Meyers

Managing Editor
Charlotte Clapp

Project Editor
Andy Beaster

Production Editor
Heather Wilkins

Indexer
Erika Millen

Technical Editor
James Kirkpatrick

Publishing Coordinator
Vanessa Evans

Interior Designer
Gary Adair

Cover Designer
Gary Adair

Contents at a Glance

Table of Contents

About the Author

Jesse Feiler has been designing databases and user-oriented solutions for two decades. He has used FileMaker since its very first incarnation on the Macintosh. He is the author of a number of books on FileMaker, the Web, Macintosh operating systems, and a variety of other technologies.

A member of the FileMaker Solutions Alliance, Jesse is also a developer of solutions for small business, non-profit organizations (particularly those in the arts fields), publishing, and production companies. Since the release of FileMaker 7, he has done a number of FileMaker rehabs of older systems. He recently began integrating FileMaker databases on Mac OS X with the new Automator technology and is busily moving data to and from InDesign and other publishing software for a variety of clients.

He has worked as a developer and manager for companies such as the Federal Reserve Bank of New York (monetary policy and bank supervision), Prodigy (early web browser), Apple (information systems), New York State Department of Health (rabies and lead poisoning), The Johnson Company (office management), and Young & Rubicam (media planning and new product development).

Active in the community, he has served on a variety of non-profit boards including those of HB Studio and Mid-Hudson Library System, as well as zoning and planning boards. Drawing in part on this experience, he is developer of MinutesMachine, the FileMaker-based tool for meeting agendas and minutes.

Jesse lives in Plattsburgh, New York. His websites are www.northcountryconsulting.com and www.philmontmill.com. Files for this book can be found at www.philmontmill.com as well as at www.samspublishing.com.

Acknowledgments

Many people have contributed to this book, not least the wonderful people at FileMaker who have developed this remarkable project over the years. In particular, Kevin Mallon and Delfina Daves have provided wonderful assistance as new versions of FileMaker have been developed.

At Sams Publishing, Betsy Brown, Acquisitions Editor, has helped to shape the book through the editorial process. It's been a pleasure to work with Scott Meyers, Andy Beaster, and Heather Wilkins who, in various ways, have helped to make the book as clear and strong as possible.

James Kirkpatrick has provided invaluable help in reviewing the technical aspects of the manuscript. His suggestions are always constructive and accurate.

At Waterside Productions, Carole McClendon has, again, provided the support and assistance so important to an author.

A number of people have helped on the projects. Many of the projects are based on real-life projects that I have worked on. In particular, Chapter 9, "Class Enrollment," is based on a much more complex enrollment system designed for HB Studio. Edith Meeks, Bernice Sobel, Felipe Bonilla, Fernando Gambaroni, Chuck Edwards, and the rest of the staff have been enormously helpful in the evolution of the full system there.

We Want to Hear from You!

As the reader of this book, *you* are our most important critic and commentator. We value your opinion and want to know what we're doing right, what we could do better, what areas you'd like to see us publish in, and any other words of wisdom you're willing to pass our way.

You can email or write me directly to let me know what you did or didn't like about this book—as well as what we can do to make our books stronger.

Please note that I cannot help you with technical problems related to the topic of this book, and that due to the high volume of mail I receive, I might not be able to reply to every message.

When you write, please be sure to include this book's title and author as well as your name and phone or email address. I will carefully review your comments and share them with the author and editors who worked on the book.

E-mail: consumer@samspublishing.com

Mail: Mark Taber
         Associate Publisher
         Sams Publishing
         800 East 96th Street
         Indianapolis, IN 46240 USA

Reader Services

For more information about this book or another Sams title, visit our website at www.samspublishing.com. Type the ISBN (excluding hyphens) or the title of a book in the Search field to find the page you're looking for.

Introduction

Over the years, FileMaker has managed to simultaneously become much more powerful and easier to use. The enormous changes in the database structure that were released in FileMaker 7 had a significant effect on many solution providers: Many of us were amazed at the amount of code we were able to remove because FileMaker itself was doing what we often had to invent for ourselves. The addition of developer features such as variables and script parameters, along with seemingly minor features such as the ability to have value lists based on numeric codes but that displayed only meaningful text labels, made our lives as developers easier and made the product even easier for users.

This book presents a collection of projects that have been built from scratch using FileMaker 7 (and sometimes FileMaker 8) features. These are not hoary old examples that have been tweaked around the edges; rather, they are ready-to-go projects that use the newest features and which, for that reason, are often much simpler than comparable FileMaker solutions from a few years ago.

In selecting and creating these projects, I have focused on a range of projects that can be of use to a variety of people in various walks of life. In addition, I have tried to find projects and aspects of projects that showcase important FileMaker features as well as some of the newest FileMaker tools. As a result, even if one or more of the projects seems like it is just what you need to use, take the time to look through other projects. You might well find interface elements that you can combine with a database design for your own, easy-to-use FileMaker solution. Likewise, if another project seems to be of no interest, it might have interface elements, scripting features, or database design ideas that will help you in other areas.

Each of the projects begins with an overview as well as a discussion of specific planning issues to be considered (general planning issues for all projects are described in Chapter 3, "Building FileMaker Solutions"). Some people skim over this material because they want to get to the FileMaker syntax and layouts. That is a mistake. In many years of developing database solutions (most of them using FileMaker) for myself, organizations I'm a part of, and for clients, I have found that the discussions about the incipient project are the most valuable part of the design process. The best planning for a project doesn't require FileMaker or even a computer. It is done in discussions—often repetitive discussions—with people who know the business best. The basic questions, "Can this ever happen?," "What do you do if that doesn't happen?," "Who makes the decision?," and so forth need to be embedded in your FileMaker solution. Beyond these questions, another set needs to be asked; basically, these questions are all a variation on "Does it have to be like that?"

In building a FileMaker solution from scratch, learning about the operation is essential to being able to create a useful solution.

During this process, one of FileMaker's most attractive features comes into play. Although the discussion doesn't require a computer, FileMaker can be a great tool for moving that discussion along. Without building the whole system, you can quickly implement a small section of a database and a small part of a layout to demonstrate how something might work. If it takes five minutes to do this, you can devote 15 minutes to the process and come up with alternatives A, B, and C. (And, in many cases, this prompts additional discussion and a consensus choice of new alternative D.)

In short, I find FileMaker one of the best tools I've ever worked with. But it is a tool. The goal (and the part of the process that I find most rewarding) is solving people's problems, transforming operations for the better, and, not least of all, learning about new businesses, meeting new people, and discovering new ways of doing things.

I hope this book helps you solve problems, develop solutions, and have just a few of the interesting adventures that I've had with FileMaker and the people who use it.

Organization of This Book

This book is divided into three parts:

▶ Part I, "Getting Started," introduces FileMaker today. FileMaker 7 included what might have been the biggest rewrite since the first release of the product. That new database format (which is used in FileMaker 8, too), brought enormous new power to the already-powerful product. If you're an old hand at FileMaker, the chapters in this part of the book will jump-start you into the world of FileMaker 7 and FileMaker 8. If you're new to FileMaker, these chapters will help put the production documentation and tutorials into perspective so you can get started with the projects in the book.

- Part II, "Projects," contains the projects that make up the bulk of this book. Each one can be used on its own or with enhancements to solve a real-world problem. In addition, a wide variety of FileMaker features are demonstrated in these projects.

- In Part III, "Appendixes," you'll find Appendix A, "FileMaker Error Codes," a handy reference to help debug FileMaker scripts you write. Appendix B, "FileMaker Resources," provides some URLs for further information about FileMaker, as well as additional resources. The glossary provides a quick reference to terms used in this book. (When you're looking for something, don't forget the index, which provides the actual page numbers of detailed descriptions of these concepts.)

Downloading the Book's Project Files

The chapter-by-chapter project and media files are available at the publisher's website, www.samspublishing.com. In addition, copies are available at the author's website, www.philmontmill.com, under the FileMaker navigation tab.

Enter this book's ISBN (0672328569) in the Search box and click Search. When the book's title is displayed, click the title to go to a page where you can download the project's files.

Conventions Used in This Book

This book uses the following conventions:

- *Italic* is used to denote key terms when they first appear in the book.

- Code lines, table names, and other code-related words are shown in `monospace text`.

TIP

Tips provide shortcuts to make your job easier or better ways to accomplish certain tasks.

NOTE

Notes provide additional information related to the surrounding topics.

CAUTION

Cautions alert you to potential problems and help you steer clear of disaster.

@work resources

- This indicates specific files that are available for download from the Sams website.

PART I: Getting Started

CHAPTER 1: Hands-On with FileMaker

Now entering its third decade, FileMaker has established a firm reputation for power and ease of use both for individuals and workgroups. Running on Mac OS X and on Windows, FileMaker organizes data rapidly and easily for users around the world. No other product provides such ease of use combined with scalability. The transition from a one-person project to a server-based application for several hundred users on a network or across the Web can be remarkably simple.

This part of the book provides an introduction to FileMaker itself. It supplements the tutorials, manuals, and examples that come with FileMaker. When a product is as easy to use as FileMaker is, it is tempting (and quite feasible) to jump in and get started. There is no reason not to do so. The three chapters in this part of the book provide some extra guidance and tie up a few loose ends that might be confusing you. Then, in the second part of the book, it is on to the details of creating projects you can use.

State-of-the-Art FileMaker

This section provides a brief overview of FileMaker today. If you're an old hand at FileMaker, you will find a brief overview of the latest and greatest features of FileMaker 8. If you are new to FileMaker, you will find a quick summary of how we got here—the two decades of FileMaker that have gone before.

FileMaker Through the Decades

There have been five major milestones in the history of FileMaker:

- The initial FileMaker product was released in March 1984. Running only on the Macintosh operating system, it provided a simple way of organizing the desktop on a single computer. It provided a logical and intuitive interface for people who wanted to organize their data without worrying about the esoterica of computer files (hence the name FileMaker). The basics of that intuitive interface remain in the current FileMaker product, although the internal workings of the software have been revised in many ways.

- Version 2, released in 1993, added support for Windows. FileMaker became the first cross-platform desktop database software product. All FileMaker products since that time have run on both Macintosh and Windows

operating systems. In addition, the FileMaker Mobile version runs on Pocket PC and the Palm OS; it provides automated synchronization with a FileMaker database running on a personal computer.

- Version 3 of FileMaker introduced relational databases in 1995. (There's more on relational databases and relationships in Chapter 3, "Building FileMaker Solutions.") A number of database products were developed at the dawn of the personal computer era. Initially, all were non-relational flat-file–based databases; only FileMaker successfully made the transition to the relational world.

- Version 4 in 1997 introduced web publishing from FileMaker, including the Instant Web Publishing feature that allows users to publish FileMaker databases and to receive updates to those databases over the Web. In versions 5 and 6 (1999 and 2002 respectively), web publishing and data sharing, including XDBC and Microsoft Office integration, were added and expanded in FileMaker. Also, limits such as file size were systematically lifted to reflect the more powerful computers available. Building on the basic database and its interface, additional features and extensions were provided.

- FileMaker 7, released in March 2004, provided a ground-up redesign of the database model while still providing compatibility with old database files. In FileMaker 7, individual database files could contain multiple tables (until that time, *database* and *table* were synonymous in FileMaker parlance).

Within a year, more than 1 million copies of FileMaker 7 were shipped.

In August 2005, FileMaker released its newest version, FileMaker 8. This product provides many new features, particularly for developers and advanced users. In addition, by exploiting the new database features introduced under the hood in FileMaker 7, FileMaker was able to provide a number of powerful and easy-to-use new features for end users, continuing the long history of such features.

This book focuses on today's FileMaker—FileMaker 8. Because the database structure for FileMaker 8 is unchanged from that of FileMaker 7, most of this book is applicable to FileMaker 7 with no modifications or changes.

The FileMaker Family of Products

There are now four basic FileMaker products:

▶ FileMaker Pro 8 is the basic product that you can use to create, modify, and query databases. It provides the features you need to not only manipulate your data but also to develop custom solutions with your own scripts and layouts. FileMaker Pro 8 enables you to share your data over a network or over the Web; up to 5 users can share your database in this way. In addition, you can use FileMaker Pro 8 to access shared FileMaker databases.

▶ FileMaker 8 Server and FileMaker Server 8 Advanced make databases available using FileMaker networking (FileMaker 8 Server) or the Web (FileMaker Server 8 Advanced), with

either Instant Web Publishing or the XML/XSLT support that is built into FileMaker. It also supports sharing through xDBC. Its restrictions are far less than those of FileMaker Pro 8: It can support up to 250 users over a network and up to 100 simultaneous users over the Web. Unlike FileMaker Pro 8, you cannot use it to create, query, or update databases—it is only a server product. Although its functionality is that of a database server, it does not need to run on a dedicated hardware server, although that might provide the most stable production environment.

▶ FileMaker Pro 8 Advanced contains all of the features of FileMaker Pro 8. In addition, it provides additional tools for the developer or advanced user. With it, you can create standalone solutions. You can also use extensive debugging tools as well as more powerful database design and scripting features that aren't provided in the basic FileMaker Pro 8 product.

▶ Finally, FileMaker Mobile, which runs on Pocket PC and Palm OS, enables you to integrate handheld devices with a database hosted with FileMaker Pro 8, FileMaker Pro 8 Advanced, or FileMaker Server. (The capability to synchronize data from a handheld device with a database hosted by FileMaker Server is new in FileMaker 8.)

Introducing the Database for This Chapter

This chapter presents the hands-on features of FileMaker—that is, those features you use directly with the mouse, keyboard, and menus as opposed to features that you use through scripts and other prepared or programmed features. In the FileMaker documentation, you'll see how to start from an empty database, create fields, enter data, report data, sort data, find data, and export data. More than two dozen Starter Solutions ship with FileMaker: They are ready for you to enter your data and get to work.

But, like any database, much of FileMaker is devoted to managing relatively large amounts of data. Starting from an empty database or an empty Starter Solution does not enable you to get a hands-on feel for using a large database. Accordingly, this chapter uses a database created from the U.S Census Bureau document titled "State Interim Population Projections by Age and Sex: 2004–2030" released April 2005 (www.census.gov/population/projections/ DownldFile4.xls), with a quarter of a million data records in it. That data consists of population projections from the U.S. Census Bureau for each state in the United States, for each age group (0–84 and 85+), and for each sex for every year from 2004 to 2030.

The data from the U.S. Census Bureau website is, in fact, an Excel spreadsheet. The database on this book's website is a FileMaker database. It is easy to convert an Excel spreadsheet to a FileMaker database (and, starting with FileMaker 8, to convert a FileMaker database to an Excel spreadsheet).

 NOTE

Many people use spreadsheets. They are a great way to organize large amounts of data, but they have a number of drawbacks. One is that their data management features are limited; another is that their sharing capabilities are extremely limited. Converting an Excel spreadsheet to a FileMaker database can provide you with a great deal of extra functionality. The conversion process is described more fully in Chapter 3. The database you download from the website has been created by using FileMaker's automated Excel spreadsheet conversion routine and a number of changes have also been made to the database design itself. Chapter 3 contains all three relevant files: the Excel spreadsheet, the database as it is after FileMaker's conversion, and the database as it is after the modification to its design that is described in Chapter 3.

Using FileMaker to Browse and Find Data

When you first open the downloaded file from the website, you see a window that looks almost but not quite like the one shown in Figure 1.1. (The difference is shown in Figure 1.2.)

@work resources

Please visit the publisher's website to access the following Chapter 1 files:

▶ **File4 normalized.fp7**

FIGURE 1.1   **Open the**
File4 normalized
database.

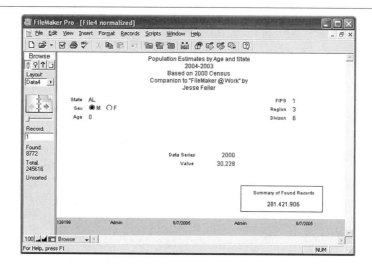

If you are running Mac OS X, the window you see is a standard Mac OS X window instead of the Windows-style window shown. The interface to FileMaker is the same on both platforms (with a very few minor exceptions that are noted in this book where relevant). Because FileMaker is platform neutral, you will find illustrations from both platforms throughout the book.

One difference between a database and other forms of stored data is that a database has no intrinsic beginning or end. (Neither does a spreadsheet in many cases, although many spreadsheet users expect their data to be presented in a certain order.)

The point of a database such as FileMaker is to store, retrieve, and manipulate data. How it is stored is, ultimately, the business of the database. What matters is that if you want the data to be presented in a certain order or if you want to see specific data items, the database must quickly do what you want so you can work with the data right away.

This particular database has been selected as an example because it is a decent size—just less than a quarter of a million records. As you explore it with FileMaker, bear that in mind. FileMaker is optimized for performance, and in most cases you will notice little if any delay in response to your FileMaker commands.

The following section provides a brief overview of FileMaker and the interface you use to manipulate data.

Using the Status Area

On the left side of the window is the *status area*. It can be shown or hidden, depending how you want it. Figure 1.2 shows the same window with the status area hidden.

To show or hide the status area, use the Status Area command from the File menu or use the Status Area button at the bottom left of the FileMaker window. Four buttons are in the lower-left corner of each window. The first on the left shows the current zoom factor (by default it is full size—100% zoom); then there are two buttons that respectively decrease or increase zoom size; the fourth from the left is the Status Area button.

FIGURE 1.2   You can hide
the status area.

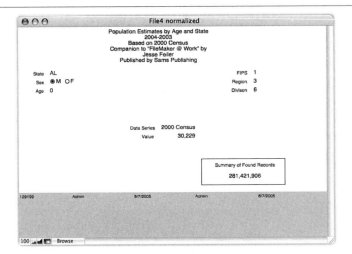

At the top of the status area are *Mode tabs* that enable you to switch quickly among FileMaker's four modes. From left to right, the Mode tabs are

- ▶ **Browse**—Browse mode enables you to view and enter data.

- ▶ **Find**—Find mode enables you to search for data.

- ▶ **Layout**—Layout mode enables you to design layouts (the graphical displays of data that people see in Browse and Find modes).

- ▶ **Preview**—Preview mode enables you to see what the current layout will look like when it is printed. It is constrained to the appropriate paper size; in addition, certain summary calculations are completed just before printing.

Each mode has its own menus and status area. For example, the Records menu appears in Browse mode; in its place, the Requests menu appears in Find mode. In Layout mode, the Layouts menu appears in

that location. That particular menu enables you to manipulate the things you are dealing with in Browse mode (records), Find mode (requests), or Layout mode (layouts).

 NOTE

Beginning with FileMaker 8, you have even more control over menus and you can rename them as you want when you create a FileMaker solution. Almost everything about FileMaker can be customized using FileMaker Pro Advanced. Remember that the default behavior is described in this book.

Browsing Data

Figure 1.1 shows the status area in Browse mode. It provides information and navigation tools to help you through the database. Beneath the Mode tabs, a drop-down menu enables you to select the layout that will be used to display the data. You might never use this drop-down menu. In the first case, not every layout is shown in the menu (as the designer, you can control that); in the second case, layouts are often part of scripts and solutions and the appropriate layout is selected for you automatically as a script runs. In addition, many FileMaker database files contain only a single layout: The drop-down menu is there, but it has no meaning because there is only one choice. (The database used in this chapter is an example of such a database. In Chapter 3, as you see how the database was developed, you will see multiple layouts in use.)

Navigation tools fill the next section of the status area. The book icon enables you to navigate one record forward or backward. The slider beneath it enables you to move rapidly through a number of records. Finally, the data entry field below the slider enables you to enter the number of the record you want to view. In the case of Figure 1.1, the first record is shown; that fact is reflected in the record number, in the position of the slider (all the way at the left), and in the book (the back arrow is dimmed).

The status area summarizes the number of records in the database as well as the number shown (that is, the number in the found set—the result of the last Find command). Finally, you can see if the database is currently sorted.

In the center of the window is the data itself. A single record is shown at a time in this view (other views are available as described later in "Using Table and List Views"). A single data record in this database consists of a single data value. That value is identified by state, sex, and age (at the upper left), as well as by a series name. Thus, the projection

for the number of men in Alabama who are under the age of one year is one of the possible values. Figures 1.1 and 1.2 show this data. The data value is 30,229. Other records show data such as the number of women in Nevada age 34 according to the 2015 estimate. (This database contains the 2000 census data as well as projections for 2004–2030).

Finding Data

You can find data with FileMaker. Finding data not only retrieves data that matches the selection criteria, but it also updates any summary information that is related to those criteria.

To find data, you enter Find mode by using the Mode tab (the magnifying glass icon second from the left at the top of the status area), the Find Mode command from the View menu, or the Mode drop-down menu at the bottom of the window (next to the Status Area button). Figure 1.3 shows Find mode.

When you enter Find mode, the data in the layout disappears. You type in the data you want to match. In the case of text data, FileMaker matches data that is similar to what you type. (The rules that govern data matching are in the FileMaker documentation as well as in the online help under Find.) In Figure 1.3, a search for data from the data series 2000 is shown.

In the status area is a Find button. When you have completed entering your search criteria, click Find, and FileMaker will find your data.

FIGURE 1.3   Use Find
mode to find data.

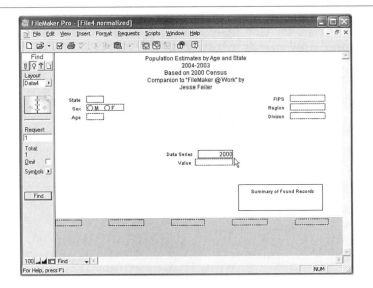

Because the default text matching is not exact, you can search for data in this database by any specific year. If you type in 2010, you will get the data for 2010 (no surprise there); however, if you look at the data, you will see that the actual series name is 2010 Pr, indicating that it is a projection. FileMaker will find the 2010 data whether you type in 2010 Pr or 2010 because 2010 is in both names. If you also have actual data for 2010 identified as 2010 Actual, searching for 2010 will find both the projected and actual data. In this database, you only have one data series for each year. For 2000 it is actual data, and for 2004–2030 it is projected data.

You can find on multiple criteria. If you want to see the data for a specific state and year, type in the two-character state code as well as the year. Then click Find and that data appears.

All of the criteria that you enter will be used to find the data. In database terminology, this is an *AND* operator—all criteria must be met.

FileMaker also supports *OR* queries. Enter criteria that you want but before clicking Find, choose Add New Request from the Requests menu. A new blank layout appears so you can enter the next set of criteria. You can enter as many requests as you want in this way. When you are done, click Find.

The rules for handling complex finds are simple:

▶ For an individual request (such as a simple find), all criteria must be met. Within a single request, FileMaker uses the AND operator on all criteria.

▶ If multiple requests are present, all criteria for each request must be met, but the found set contains the results for all of the requests. In other words, if Request 1 finds 5 records, and Request 2 finds 10 records, you might have up to 15 records in the found set. (You might have less than 15 records because the requests might refer to the same records.) For multiple requests, FileMaker uses the OR operator.

In Find mode, the status area enables you to page through the various requests you have created before you click Find. In this way, you can modify complex finds.

You can work with found sets in other ways. If you have found some data, you can expand that found set or search within it. After a find is completed, you will normally be back in Browse mode. If you want to refine your request, return to Find mode and choose Constrain Found Set or Expand Found Set from the Requests menu. In the case of Constrain Found Set, the follow-on find searches within the found set; in the case of Expand Found Set, the follow-on find adds its results to the found set.

Summary fields that are part of the database are updated to reflect the appropriate values based on the current found set. If you refer to Figure 1.1 or 1.2, you will see that the summary field in the lower right of the layout has a value of 281,421,906.

Sorting Data

FileMaker makes it easy to sort data. In Browse mode, choose Sort Records from the File menu. You can select the fields you want to sort on, and you can specify the sort order for each—ascending, descending, or a custom order (that will be based on a value list you have defined).

 TIP

When you construct a database, remember that people see the names of your fields when they sort data. Naming fields accurately and descriptively makes it easier for people to get the most of your database.

Double-check the Numbers

Develop the habit of checking summary data, such as the total of 281,421,906. That number is the summary of all records for 2000 (the actual census numbers). That number is not merely the value of the total as computed by FileMaker; it is the number of people in the United States on April 1, 2000, as enumerated by the Census Bureau. (The methodology is detailed at www.census.gov.)

Whether you are learning FileMaker and want to make certain that you are formulating Find commands correctly or you are developing a custom solution, make it a habit to check your results against known benchmarks such as these. You might say that your data *matches* known data, *foots* to it, or *equals* it. However you phrase it, hold on to any known values like this to check your work.

That particular value—the population of the United States—is a valuable benchmark because it is an externally verified value (such as a bank account balance). Also useful are numbers that are internal to FileMaker. For example, the status area in Figure 1.1 indicates that 8,772 records have been found. That is the number of records for any year's data in this database. You can double-check that value to make certain that it is correct by performing the following calculation:

2 sexes

× 51 states (50 states and the District of Columbia)

× 86 age groups (0–84, 85+)

Use numbers like these to check your work. For example, if you do not have 8,772 records for any given year, you have made a mistake either in database logic or in typing.

Sorting is essential for making reports function properly if they have subtotals. The data must be sorted properly so the subtotals for each level are properly calculated. (More on this is found later in this chapter in the section on creating reports in "Using FileMaker Layout Mode.")

Many people sort their data too much. A database is designed to quickly locate data. Do you want to locate the data for all states with a state code that starts with N? In Find mode, type N or N*—the * symbol indicates zero or more characters. Do you want to find all records for people with ages that end in 9? Type #9—the # symbol means one digit. You can combine these symbols as needed. Figure 1.4 shows the Find symbols.

FIGURE 1.4   **Use symbols to construct find requests.**

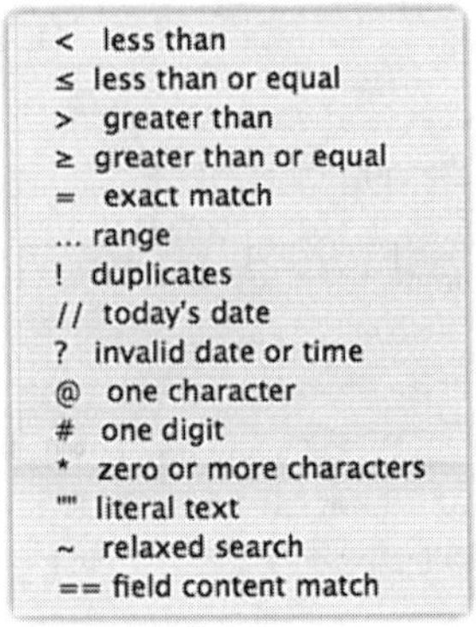

```
<    less than
≤    less than or equal
>    greater than
≥    greater than or equal
=    exact match
...  range
!    duplicates
//   today's date
?    invalid date or time
@    one character
#    one digit
*    zero or more characters
""   literal text
~    relaxed search
==   field content match
```

Because it is so easy to locate data, you might find that it is unnecessary to sort the database as much as you might first think. The most useful process for most people is to use Find to produce a found set of records and then to constrain that found set to home in on records that interest you.

Alternatively, you can sort the database, and then step through the records in whatever order you have sorted them. This tends to take more computer time. On a single computer, it does not matter very much, but with a shared database, excessive sorting can adversely affect performance. For reports,

though, you might need to sort the database, as you will see in the projects later in this book.

Using Data Entry Fields

Data entry fields in FileMaker work just as they do in other applications. Depending on how the layout has been set up, you can type in text, use drop-down menus or lists, radio buttons, or check boxes. In FileMaker 8, type-ahead data entry is supported: You can start to type data and FileMaker will provide you with a drop-down list of previously entered values that match what you have typed.

Perhaps the most important aspect of data entry that you need to know is that starting in FileMaker 7, you can insert any file into a FileMaker database. If a field is defined as a container (a field that can contain a file), you can insert a movie or picture into it. You can select the field, choose File from the Insert menu, and then navigate to whatever file you want to insert. The dialog enables you to choose whether to insert the file itself or a reference to the file. If you insert the file, your database will be correspondingly larger (it includes the file); with a reference, you will save database space, but the reference will break if you move the file. A companion menu command from the Edit menu, Export Field Contents, enables you to export the contents of a container field. Thus, you can place a file into a database and later move it elsewhere when you export it. Remember that this can result in large databases and slow network performance, but when used properly it can be a powerful extension to FileMaker. You will see a container field used in Chapter 7, "Managing Production, Tasks, and Subtasks."

Exporting FileMaker Data

You can export data from FileMaker using the Export Records command from the File menu. That command opens a dialog that enables you to choose the fields to export and their export formats. In FileMaker 8, you now have the option to automatically create and send an email message with the exported file attached.

As shown in Figure 1.5, the Export Records dialog enables you to choose from a variety of standard data formats; you also can export the data as a new FileMaker database or as an Excel spreadsheet. In addition, you can export fields only from the current layout or table, not from the entire database.

FIGURE 1.5   **Export data in a variety of formats.**

Using Table and List Views

In the figures seen so far in this chapter, the data is shown in Form view. Form view shows a single data record at a time using the current layout.

List view uses the appropriate layout, but more than one record can be shown at a time. Depending on the size of the window and the layout, you might be able to see more than one record at a time; alternatively,

an individual record might be taller than the window and you cannot see even one at a time. In List view, a small black indicator at the left shows you which record is current. In addition, the record number in the status area shows you at which record you are looking.

Table view displays the data in a spreadsheet-like display. If the database designer has set the options to allow it, you can reorder columns by dragging them back and forth; also, clicking in a column header sorts the column.

You will see Table and List views in the projects later in this book. Many people only use Form view. If you are not familiar with the other views, experiment with them (they are in the Views menu in Browse mode).

 NOTE

Form, List, and Table views are available in both Browse and Find mode.

Using FileMaker Layout Mode

Layout mode enables you to design the interface for your solution. Unlike Browse and Find modes that allow you to view the data by form, table, or list, Layout mode is a totally different mode, one which enables you to draw graphical elements and organize data entry fields using tools that are generally similar to those in any graphical drawing application. Figure 1.6 shows the Layout mode with the design tools in the status area.

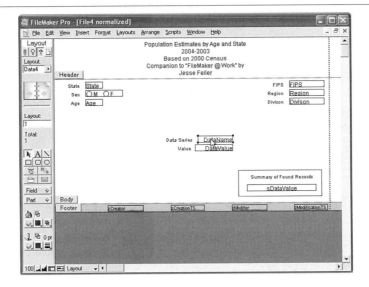

Creating a Layout with FileMaker's Assistance

In Layout mode, the Records menu (Browse mode) and the Requests menu (Find mode) is called the Layouts menu in Layout mode. As with the others, it enables you to create, delete, and control the objects that you deal with (layouts, in this case). If you choose New Layout from the Layouts menu, you can have FileMaker walk you through a variety of prepared layouts for printed reports, interactive data entry, and even labels. If you use these default layouts, you can go back and modify them afterward.

Using FileMaker Fields in Layout Mode

In addition to the graphical tools, you can add fields to a layout in Layout mode. To do so, drag the Field icon from the status area to the approximate location where you want the field; when you release the mouse button, you are prompted to choose the field you want on the layout.

The projects in Part II of this book walk you through the process of designing various interfaces. The basic tools of the Layout mode that are located in the status area are described in the online help as well as in the documentation that comes with FileMaker. If you are not familiar with them, take a few moments to explore the Layout mode. Select fields and graphical elements; use the pen and fill controls to change their appearance. You will find that these behave as you would expect. The FileMaker-specific layout tools (such as the ability to create tab controls) are described in this book as they are needed in the projects.

Layouts enable you to combine fields from several tables in a variety of ways. This brief overview addresses the most general case—adding fields to a layout from an as-yet undefined table. As you progress through the projects, you will see how to use advanced techniques, including portals and related tables, to make your layouts more complex and powerful.

The Format menu, shown in Figure 1.7, enables you to set various attributes of the field, such as font, size, and style. In addition, the Field/Control submenu enables you to manage FileMaker-specific attributes.

FIGURE 1.7   Use the Field/Control submenu to set FileMaker-specific attributes.

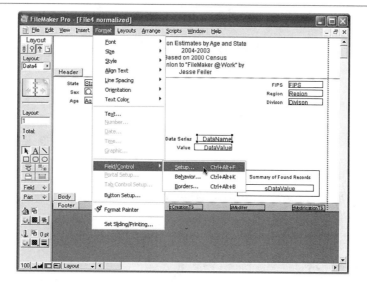

When you have selected a field in Layout mode, you can also use a contextual menu to set attributes. As shown in Figure 1.8, the contextual menu for a selected field includes items from the Format menu as well as access to controls on the status area (such as fill and pen patterns).

In the Field/Control submenu, you can specify the type of field that is shown in the layout. Figure 1.9 shows how you can implement a type-ahead feature starting in FileMaker 8.

Figure 1.9 also shows a Drop-down Calendar option that you can use for date fields. These and other specific FileMaker data entry and display features are demonstrated throughout the projects.

FIGURE 1.8   Contextual menus for selected data fields enable you to access the formatting commands.

FIGURE 1.9   The auto-
complete feature saves
keystrokes and improves data
quality by using previously
entered values.

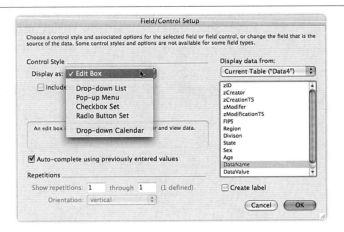

Finally, the Field Behavior controls shown in Figure 1.10 enable you to control whether a field is modifiable in Browse or Find mode. This enhancement was implemented in FileMaker 7. Many designers make almost all of the data entry fields editable in Find mode (so that you can, for example, find on the date of data entry) while making only a few of them modifiable in Browse mode.

FIGURE 1.10   Define how a field can be changed with the Field Behavior dialog.

Using Layout Parts

Layouts can contain multiple *layout parts*. A layout part contains graphics and data elements from any of the available database tables. From a practical standpoint, a part is significant because it can contain summary fields when the data is sorted in a specific order. You will see how to use layout parts and summaries in the projects in Part II.

Creating Reports

To get a jump on the projects in Part II, you can use the New Layout command to create a report. Using the defaults, explore the creation of reports with subtotals. Make certain you choose the option to create a script to run the report. What you will have is a report that relies on the data being sorted in a specific manner—and a script that sorts the data in the necessary way. Many people find it easiest to use the default report templates to create a basic report and to then use the layout tools to modify the report.

Using FileMaker Preview Mode

The last of the four FileMaker modes is Preview mode. Preview mode displays the data as it will be printed. As you can see in Figure 1.11, a dotted line shows the printable borders of the selected paper. Some layout elements, such as a footer, are placed to the bottom of the page—not the window.

FIGURE 1.11 Layout mode shows reports as they will appear when printed.

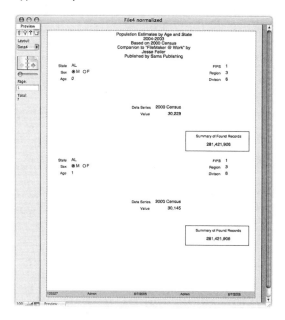

In Preview mode, buttons do not work: What you are seeing is what will be printed. Preview mode also updates summary data for the printed report. You can display data in Preview mode on the screen, and, in fact, if you have summary fields in a layout, you might need to do so for the summaries to be properly updated.

CHAPTER 2: Automating FileMaker

In Chapter 1, "Hands-On with FileMaker," you saw many FileMaker features you can use interactively. In this chapter, you explore some of the automation tools in FileMaker. These tools—primarily scripts and calculations—enable you to set up FileMaker to run on its own or, at the least, to perform automated functions without your needing to point and click your way through menus and commands.

For most people, developing FileMaker custom solutions means using scripts and calculations (as described in this chapter) as well as layouts and advanced database design features (as described in Chapter 3, "Building FileMaker Solutions"). With these tools, you can produce a customized solution as sophisticated and powerful as you want.

Without these tools, you still have FileMaker itself along with the Starter Solutions that come in the package. You do not have to create anything unless you want to. Further, you can develop a customized solution that relies solely on the basics of FileMaker, never bothering with scripts, calculations, layouts, or advanced database design features. But with not too much effort, you can create a customized solution that does exactly what you and your business need done.

Introducing ScriptMaker

Scripts are the basic programming language of FileMaker. FileMaker's scripting language is its own—you do not have to learn (or brush up on) a programming language such as Java, C++, or the like. Even better, you do not have to remember FileMaker's scripting syntax because you never type a single line of script. Using ScriptMaker, the script authoring tool built into FileMaker, you point at the script steps you want to use, click on them, and then specify parameters with the same point-and-click interface. That means no mismatched sets of quotation marks, no commas in the wrong place, and no misspelled words. (In all fairness, if you try hard enough you can manage to misalign the If and End If statements, and you can manage to produce some other errors, but by and large, your script errors are errors of logic, not of typography or spelling.)

Writing a Basic Script

Scripts enable you to automate many of the interactive FileMaker commands, such as performing a find, setting a field to a value, or showing and hiding the status area. They also enable you to implement commands that have no interactive parallel, such as managing how FileMaker handles errors that

occur during processing. ScriptMaker is the built-in tool you use to create scripts. It is described in the online documentation and help; in this chapter you will find an overview of its features as well as an in-depth look at some of its more powerful features.

To begin working with FileMaker scripts, use the Script menu to open ScriptMaker. The initial window shows you the scripts in your database file; you can use the buttons to create new scripts as shown in Figure 2.1.

FIGURE 2.1   Start creating and editing your scripts with ScriptMaker.

Double-clicking a script name (or selecting it and clicking the Edit button) enables you to begin editing it as shown in Figure 2.2.

At the left, the various ScriptMaker steps are displayed. They can be organized alphabetically or categorically. You will note that with each successive release of FileMaker, more script steps are provided.

FIGURE 2.2   The
ScriptMaker window provides
editing tools.

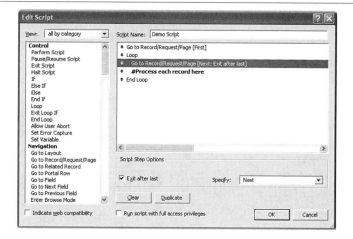

Because FileMaker now can run over the Web with web browsers as the interface, it is important to note that some script steps are not available. The check box at the lower left dims out the script steps that are not compatible with the Web. In general, these are interface-related script steps; the FileMaker menus are not available to Web users because they are using a web browser, not FileMaker.

To create a script, select the script step you want to use and double-click it; it moves to the script at the right of the window shown in Figure 2.2. Alternatively, select the script step and click the Move button that appears at the bottom of the window to move the script step into the script.

You can reorder script steps by dragging them up or down with the double-headed arrows that appear at the left of each script step. Some script steps require further specification. Those specifications are typically represented in the script by commands in square brackets, such as [First] in the first line of the script shown in Figure 2.2).

In order to set these specifications, highlight the script step involved and use the area at the bottom of the window to enter or select the data you want. In Figure 2.2, for example, the Go to Record/Request/Page script step is highlighted; in the Script Step Options area at the bottom of the window, you can choose to go to the first record, the last record, or the next record. The Next option is chosen; when it is, a check box at the left enables you to specify that FileMaker should exit after the last record.

The script shown in Figure 2.2 is a typical script (or section of a script). It goes to the first record, it loops through each succeeding record, and then it exits after the last record. Here, you will notice that a boldface comment is inserted indicating where the actual processing should be done. As you will see if you experiment, adding a comment is just like adding any other script step: You find it in the list at the left, and then you double-click it (or click Move) to add it to the script. Script step options for the Comment script step enable you to specify the text of the comment. If you have not worked with ScriptMaker, try doing so for a few minutes. You will see how easy it is. If you are used to a programming or scripting language in which you type commands, it might take you a moment to get used to the point-and-click interface; however, you will quickly adjust and be grateful for the lack of syntax errors this interface guarantees.

Designing a Script Architecture

Creating a script with ScriptMaker is very simple. Designing an architecture for the scripts in your FileMaker solution is more of a challenge—to a large extent, that is what this book is about. This section provides you with an overview of scripting guidelines and architecture. You might be chomping at the bit wanting to get started, but understanding how best to organize your solution and its scripts saves you time and effort as well as contributing to the quality of your FileMaker solution.

In the early days of FileMaker scripting, it was possible just to think of scripts as ways to automate the hands-on use of FileMaker. Today, scripting is much more advanced; it makes possible the development of the powerful FileMaker solutions that help people run their businesses. In addition to understanding the FileMaker script steps, you should understand how best to design your scripts. Many of the principles proposed in this section are not unique to FileMaker. They borrow heavily from best practices of modern system development, including the concepts of object-oriented programming. Do not let this sophisticated background intimidate you—the principles are quite simple.

Design Scripts for Readability and Reuse

Many traditional IT projects start with a lengthy design and review process that is followed by implementation and formalized testing. After that, the system is more or less frozen (until the next version goes through the same process).

FileMaker projects, on the other hand, tend to evolve gradually. This is due in part to the characteristics of people and organizations that use FileMaker as well as to the ease with which changes can be made. One consequence of this continuing process of evolution is that you might not know exactly how your scripts (as well as databases, layouts, and the like) will be used. Protect your investment in analysis and implementation by making your scripts easy to understand. At the simplest level, that means using comments. Good scripts have two sets of comments:

- A comment at the beginning of the script can describe the purpose of the script as well as assumptions that it makes (the database table is sorted, the layout is shown in Browse mode, and so forth).

- Sections of scripts are identified by comments indicating what they do. For example, a comment preceding a Loop statement can tell you that the loop handles all unprocessed transactions.

Instead of (or in addition to) comments, you can make your scripts easy to understand by splitting them up into small, clearly-defined scripts. If the scripts are clearly named, their purposes are obvious. Figure 2.3 shows the scripts in the database used in this chapter and in Chapter 1. You can see that the data conversion scripts are clearly identified.

FIGURE 2.3   Use clearly identified scripts to show what is happening.

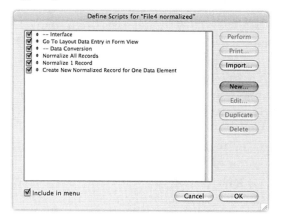

It is common and good practice to use empty scripts (that is, scripts with nothing but a name) to organize the list of scripts in ScriptMaker. As Figure 2.3 shows, there are two groups of scripts—those dealing with the interface and those dealing with data conversion.

 NOTE

The data conversion process performs a process known as normalization. For now, you need not worry about what that process entails. It is described in detail in Chapter 3. Note, too, that the scripts in this part of the chapter are presented to demonstrate architectural and design issues; do not worry about the syntax of specific script steps.

Make Scripts Atomic: Do One Clearly Identified Thing with No Side Effects

The clearly named data conversion scripts in `File4 Normalized.fp7` call one another as their titles suggest. Normalize All Records is a simple script that loops through all records; for each one, it calls Normalize 1 Record.

Normalize 1 Record, in turn, normalizes each of the data elements in a single record by repeatedly calling Create New Normalized Record for One Data Element.

Because each script is clearly labeled as to its purpose, and because each script does only one thing, a single glance shows what is going on. As a result, it is not even necessary to annotate scripts like these with comments.

Making a script atomic and self-contained means more than just keeping it confined to a single, simple purpose. It also means that the script relies on other scripts and data conditions to a minimal extent. For example, most of these scripts begin by setting the layout as necessary; in their final lines, they restore the layout to what it was when the script started executing. Thus, these scripts do what they claim to do with no extraneous actions (such as leaving the database layout set to something other than what it was when the script began).

NOTE

ScriptMaker formats its scripts automatically in its own window. For the sake of clarity, FileMaker scripts shown as text in this book are reformatted and realigned as appropriate to make them easier to read. You cannot necessarily reproduce the spacing shown in these code listings using ScriptMaker.

Factor Your Scripts: Keep the Interface Separate

In addition to focusing scripts on a specific well-identified task, bear in mind that scripts should be divided into those that might involve user interaction and those that do not. This is called *factoring*. Often, pairs of scripts are used to handle a specific task.

The first script of such a pair is full of interaction. Custom dialogs often abound. The code has many If steps that test for data conditions as well as for the Cancel button in a custom dialog. Here is one such loop; it is based on the Class Enrollment project in Chapter 9, "Implementing a Scheduling Solution." It keeps looping until valid data is entered or the Cancel button is pressed. At the end of this loop (and others), another script is performed that has no user interaction at all.

```
Loop
  Show Custom Dialog
    [ Title: "Enrollment";
    Message: "Enter the class code.";
    Buttons: "OK", "Cancel";
    Input #1:
      Class Lookups::gClass Code,
        "Class Code";
    Input #2:
      Class Lookups::gTerm, "Term" ]

  #Cancel
  If [ Get (LastMessageChoice)=2 ]
    Go to Layout [original layout]
    Exit Script [   ]
  End If
Commit Records/Requests
Exit Loop If
  [ classes::Course  ≠"" ]

  Show Custom Dialog [ Title: "Error";
    Message:
      "Invalid class name or code.";
    Buttons: "Try Again", "Cancel" ]

  #Cancel
  If [ Get ( LastMessageChoice ) = 2 ]
    Go to Layout [ original layout ]
    Exit Script [   ]
  End If

  #Try Again
End Loop
```

No Interaction Means No Interaction—Set Error Capture

Even if your intention is to use your solution interactively, separating the interface from the scripts that do the actual updates means that at some point in the future you can easily convert your solution to allow batch processing at night or at a remote location. And before you think that you will never do such a thing, remember that interaction with users using custom dialogs in FileMaker is not supported on the Web. If you decide to publish your database on the Web, you will be able to use your noninteractive scripts, but you will need to replace the interactions that use custom dialogs.

It is not hard to separate your use of custom dialogs from other processing, but you also need to remember to catch dialogs that FileMaker might use. More than ever, it is important to use the Set Error Capture script step.

Set Error Capture can be set to on or off. Typically, the script step is used twice in a script. At the beginning it is set to on, and at the end it is set to off (its default value).

When Error Capture is on, FileMaker suppresses most of its dialogs and warning messages—it just plugs ahead. This eliminates user interaction, but it also can allow your script to jump the tracks when it encounters unanticipated events.

The usual procedure is to turn Error Capture on, and then to use Get (LastError) to check if an error occurred after every script step that could generate an error. (Get (LastError) along with other Get functions is described in the online help documentation.) More than 75 functions enable you to get everything from the last error, the current date, and the button clicked in a custom dialog. If an error is found, you must handle it yourself.

The fullest implementation of this structure is something like the following:

```
Set Error Capture [on]
# Do something
If (Get (LastError) = 1
   #handle error -1
Else If (Get (LastError) = 2
   #handle error 2
Else
   #handle more errors
#Process the next script step and
   check for errors.
```

In practice, you can generally decide which of the scores of errors you want to check for; the number is usually manageable. Some of the errors can be dismissed right away because they cannot logically occur (error 3—Command is unavailable, for instance). If the script has been tested, many of the error codes in the 100s cannot occur because the tables and files will be present. Other codes (including some in that range) might occur and might not be errors; finding no records is not necessarily an error. In fact, it might be a desired result.

Often, there are only two error conditions you care about: 0 (no error) and anything else. If the result of a script step is not 0, you might want to simply terminate the script.

Whatever you do, don't give in and put up a dialog from within a supposedly noninteractive script. You will see ways of handling the issue of reporting script results in the various projects.

The FileMaker error codes and their descriptions are shown in Appendix A, "FileMaker Error Codes."

Exploring ScriptMaker Features

As noted, with each release of FileMaker, a few new script steps are added. In some cases, such as the capability to export using the Excel format, the new script steps represent new functionality. In other cases, the new script steps implement functionality that applies only to scripts. If you are familiar with FileMaker, most of the script steps will be familiar to you from your interactive use of the application. Likewise, if you are familiar with ScriptMaker in versions of FileMaker before version 8, script steps will be familiar to you in many ways. And in some ways, there will be welcome new functionality to learn.

Until version 8, the FileMaker product line included FileMaker Developer. That product is now part of FileMaker Advanced, the tool that provides you with script debugging and maintenance features as well as advanced ScriptMaker tools.

Two of the most important new features are the capability to disable script steps and the capability to cut and paste them between and among scripts.

Disabling Script Steps

The ScriptMaker window in FileMaker Advanced is shown in Figure 2.4.

To disable script steps, select them and click the Disable button as shown in Figure 2.4. (If the button is not visible, you are running FileMaker, not FileMaker Advanced.)

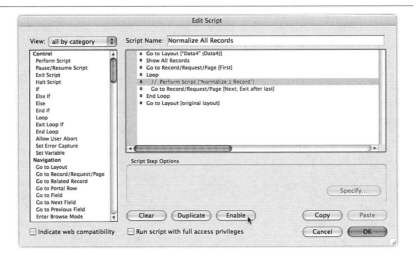

FIGURE 2.4   Disable script steps and copy or paste them from the buttons below Script Step Options in FileMaker Advanced.

This welcome addition is a help in debugging scripts. You can disable script steps you are not sure about while you debug others. Alternatively, you can disable script steps that you know are incomplete (perhaps a database file does not yet exist), but you will have them ready for enabling at a later time. You can accomplish the same goal by inserting a comment, but you need to type the comment and indicate what script step was or will be there.

Cutting and Pasting Script Steps

Copying and pasting script steps work in a similar way: Select the step or steps you want to copy, and then click Copy. In the script to which you want to paste them (the same script, another script in the same database file, or a script in another file), click on the step just before the location where you want to paste the copied script steps.

This is a welcome addition, but it is not foolproof. You can paste script steps from one database file to another, and, in doing so, you can create references to undefined tables,

layouts, or scripts (that were in the first file). FileMaker will do its best to fix the scripts, but, just as with imported scripts, you need to check your imported and pasted scripts and script steps to make certain that their references are still valid.

Using Control Script Steps

Some people skip over most of the control script steps. Perform Script enables you to do just that—perform a script from another script, and it is frequently used. But the others sometimes seem too "programmer-y." If you have been hesitant to use them, it is time to have another look. With FileMaker's new scripting features, you have a world-class programming tool, and you might as well use its world-class features.

Two sets of control script steps are commonly used in many programming languages: conditional (If) statements and loop (repeat) statements. In addition, with FileMaker 8, a new control script step, Set Variable has been added. It is a significant addition to this category of script steps.

Conditional (If) Script Steps

Conditional statements are among the most common of programming constructs. If one condition is true, certain code is executed; if another condition is true, other code is executed; and if neither is true, a third set of code is executed. Variations on this pattern abound.

Conditional script steps intuitively make sense—human beings make such choices all the time. If the coffee cup is low, the waiter might top it off, but if it is filled to the brim, the waiter will not give it a second glance. However, conditional statements often hide the power of databases. In a manual process, a clerk might check each account in turn; if there is money owing, a bill is sent, but if there is no outstanding balance, nothing is sent. Further, if there is a credit balance, perhaps a letter is sent asking if a refund is desired.

With a database, it is much simpler to push that decision-making process into the database. In this scenario, you could set up two database queries. The first would retrieve all accounts with money owing; the second would retrieve all accounts with a credit balance. The accounts with no balance would never be retrieved.

This process is simple to implement. It involves constructing a query (often a complex one), retrieving the data, and then doing exactly the same thing to every record that has been retrieved. Instead of coding If statements in a script, you code find requests.

In designing your scripts, look for ways in which you can avoid If statements by processing all records that fulfill certain criteria and then looping through them. From a manual point of view, this would be

inefficient, but when working with a database, it is remarkably efficient. And, as an added benefit, the code that you write is easy to read. (If statements within If statements within If statements are notoriously difficult to read and debug.)

Loop (Repeat) Script Steps

Loop script steps are most often used to loop through the records that have been generated by a Find script step. The process is generally the same:

1. You perform a find to get the records.

2. If any records have been returned, go to the first record.

3. Within a loop, process a record.

4. Then go to the next record.

5. Exit the loop after the last record.

No other steps are involved.

If you have used the logic described in the previous section (getting all of the records fulfilling certain criteria as described in "Conditional (If) Script Steps"), you will know that each record you retrieve must be treated exactly the same as every other record. One consequence of this design is that the sequence of records being processed does not matter: They are all to be handled the same way.

Two common inefficiencies in FileMaker scripts are unnecessary sorting of records in this type of operation (there is no need to sort if they are all handled the same way) and testing explicitly for record numbers or other signs that the last record has been reached. The Go to Next Record script step provides a check box at the left that exits the enclosing loop after the last record. FileMaker handles it all for you automatically.

Using Variables in FileMaker Scripts

With FileMaker 8, variables have been added to ScriptMaker. Together with script parameters, which were added in FileMaker 7, they make the ScriptMaker tools a match for most scripting and programming languages.

A database stores data in fields within records (as you will see in Chapter 3, sometimes the terminology is columns within rows—as in a spreadsheet—but the concept is the same). Each record has the same fields as every other record in a database table, although generally the data values are different from one record to another.

There has always been a need in FileMaker to handle data that does not fit into the strict database model. Single values unrelated to a specific record (such as a sales tax rate), are often required in a database or a FileMaker solution. The way of handling this has traditionally been to create *global fields*—fields that have a single value for all records in the database. Global fields appear in each record (so in this case each record has a sales tax field), but only one value is stored in the database for every record to access.

With FileMaker 8, variables are introduced to scripting. A variable has a name, and you can set a value for it either directly or as the result of a calculation. Variable names start with $ or with $$. A local variable—a variable that is available within a single script—starts with $. A global variable—a variable that is available to all scripts within a database file—starts with $$. You will see variables used in the projects later in this book.

Committing and Reverting Records

Starting with FileMaker 7, the Commit/Revert control script step was implemented. In database parlance, committing refers to the process of writing a set of changes to disk as if they all happened at once. For example, in filling in a layout for a contact, you might enter the name, address, and telephone number; none of that data is necessarily in the database until the record is committed. Most of the time, you commit a record interactively by moving to a new record, closing its window, or doing something else that indicates to FileMaker that you are done with the data entry process for a single record.

For a variety of reasons (not least of which is that a single record can be visible in several windows at the same time), it became necessary in FileMaker 7 to allow a script writer to explicitly commit records (or to discard a set of changes by reverting the record). Until FileMaker 7, it was possible to commit records using a variety of ad hoc methods (going to another record and then returning to the primary record, going into Find mode and then back to Browse mode, and so forth), but now there is an explicit Commit command. Get in the habit of committing changes when you have finished them. (Your scripts might work without commit steps, but as they are modified they might break.)

Debugging Scripts

Now that FileMaker scripting is more powerful than ever, it becomes necessary not only to plan the architecture of your scripts but also to carefully debug them. Many strategies can be employed here.

First, remember the pointers for developing well-designed scripts. Scripts that are self-contained and that do one thing are easy to debug: You can review them by reading them, and often that is all that is necessary. But when you start putting scripts together, and if you are trying to make sense of complex scripts written in the past by others, you need additional tools.

One way of debugging scripts is to insert Pause script steps; while the script is paused you can look to see what is happening. You are limited to the variables you can see in the current layout, so many people insert Custom Dialog script steps to display relevant dialogs.

All of these techniques will help you, but for true debugging, you need the Script Debugger that is found in FileMaker Advanced (FileMaker Developer in FileMaker 7 and earlier).

You access the debugger from the Tools menu. Turn it on by selecting Debug Scripts. A check mark appears next to the menu command, but nothing happens until you run a script. As soon as a script runs, the debugger window, shown in Figure 2.5, opens.

FIGURE 2.5 **Use the Script Debugger to help resolve issues with scripts.**

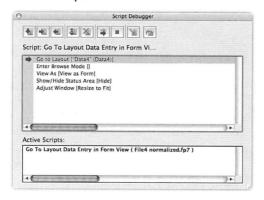

Your script is in the main window of the script debugger. An arrow points to the next script step that will be executed. At the top of the window, buttons enable you to control the debugger. (You can also control the debugger from the Debugging Controls submenu in the Tools menu; those commands also have keyboard equivalents.)

From the left, the buttons in the debugger window are

- **Step**—This button causes the next script step to execute. The debugger then pauses.

- **Step Into**—If the next script step is a Perform Script step, stepping with the Step button will perform that script step (that is, the script that is performed) and then pause at the next script step in the main script. However, Step Into goes into the performed script and pauses at the first step. You can then step through the performed step. After the last step, you are returned to the main script.

- **Step Out Of**—If you have stepped into a subscript, stepping out of the subscript continues executing that subscript and stops on the first step of the main script after the subscript has completed processing.

- **Run**—This starts the script running from wherever it is stopped; it continues either to the end of the script or to a breakpoint (described later in this section).

- **Halt Script**—This button stops the script and closes the Script Debugger window. Use this to jump out of a script when you realize that it has gone off the track, or when you have seen what you need to do to modify the script so it works as you want it to work.

- ▶ **Set Next Step**—Highlight a script step and then click Set Next Step. The arrow now points to the script step you selected, and the Step button (or any of the other step or run buttons) executes this step as the next step. You jump over any intervening steps. If you know that you will want to jump over some steps in a script, consider disabling those steps in ScriptMaker rather than setting the next step each time you run the script.

- ▶ **Set/Clear Breakpoint**—A *breakpoint* is a script step at which the debugger stops. You can set a breakpoint in ScriptMaker by clicking in the margin to the left of the script step or by highlighting a script step in the debugger and clicking Set/Clear Breakpoint. (If a breakpoint is already set for that step, clicking the button removes it.) When a breakpoint is set, the script stops just before that line is executed.

- ▶ **ScriptMaker**—This button opens the script in ScriptMaker so you can modify it while it is running.

- ▶ **Data Viewer**—This button opens the Data Viewer that is described in the following section.

Using Data Viewer

Data Viewer is available only in FileMaker Advanced. It enables you to monitor values of fields, expressions, and variables as your scripts are executing. Open the Data Viewer from the Tools menu or from the script debugger. The Data Viewer is shown in Figure 2.6.

Use the buttons in the lower right of the window to add and remove expressions from the Data Viewer. Figure 2.7 shows how you can specify an item to evaluate in the Data Viewer, either once or repeatedly. Notice that you can construct full expressions.

FIGURE 2.6 Use the Data Viewer to help debug your scripts and solutions.

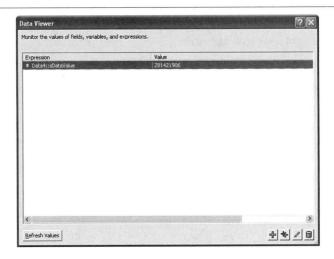

FIGURE 2.7 **Evaluate expressions with the Data Viewer.**

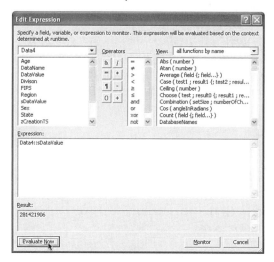

Using Script Parameters

In the scripts shown previously in this chapter, you saw extensive use of script parameters. These were new in FileMaker 7, and they make it possible to write complex and highly structured scripts that adhere to the best programming standards.

A script parameter is a value that is passed into a script when it is invoked. If you are attaching a script to an interface element, you can specify the script parameter at that time as described in Chapter 3. Alternatively, if you are performing a script from within another script, you can pass in a script parameter when you create the Perform Script script step.

There can only be one script parameter passed into a script, but it can contain a number of values. Thus, you will see the creation of multivalue script parameters and their subsequent unpacking. For example, here is how a script parameter with eight

values is created and passed into the Perform Script script step:

```
Perform Script [ "Create New Normalized
  Record for One Data Element";
  Parameter: File4::FIPS & ¶ &
    File4::Region & ¶ &
    File4::Division & ¶ &
    File4::State & ¶ &
    File4::Sex & ¶ &
    File4::Age & ¶ &
    "2004 Pr" & ¶ &
    File4::Projection 2004 ]
```

Values are separated by the ¶ character that you can find in the calculation window (described in the "Using Calculations" section). Spacing does not matter in creating the script parameter, but for readability, it is easiest to place each value of the script parameter on its own line.

When a script executes with a script parameter, it can use the Get (ScriptParameter) function to retrieve the script parameter. If the parameter has multiple values, you can split it apart as in the following code:

```
Set Field [ Data4::FIPS;
  Left (MiddleValues
    (Get (ScriptParameter) ; 1 ; 1);
      Length (MiddleValues
        (Get (ScriptParameter) ; 1 ; 1))
      - 1) ]
```

Each of the values in a multivalue script parameter ends with the ¶ symbol. As a result, when you are splitting the parameter apart, you need to use the Left function to retrieve all except the last character (¶) of each value. The MiddleValues function retrieves the entire nth value, on which you will then use the Left function. Note in the code shown here that the final line does not need to use the Left function because the

GetAsNumber function (which is used when you are certain that you are unpacking a number) drops non-numeric characters such as ¶ automatically.

Using Calculations

As you saw in Figure 2.7, it is possible to create expressions in FileMaker. These can be expressions to be evaluated in the Data Viewer or calculations that are stored in the database as calculation fields. Calculations are a powerful extension to the basic database functionality of FileMaker. You will see them used extensively in the projects in Part II of this book.

Many people approach calculations in a purely mathematic sense—given a unit price and a quantity, a calculation can multiply the two values together to get a total price. That is a very common use of calculations.

But you can do much, much more with calculations, bringing them into the realm of scripting amidst the notion of not having to do everything manually with a point-and-click interface.

For example, consider using calculations to perform edits. A general approach to edits and error-checking is procedural, checking to see if the values are appropriate. The disadvantage to this is that you as the script writer need to remember to perform these edits. You can create calculations that automatically do the edits for you every time they are needed. Here is a scenario that is used several times in this book.

In Chapter 9 a solution is presented that helps handle class enrollment. One of the issues is that each class has a maximum number of students that can be enrolled. The number of students enrolled in a given class can be found in a variable, sEnrollmentCount. (Note that this example is simplified from the code that you will find in Chapter 9.) Another variable, MaxClassSize, represents the number of students the class can handle. A calculation checks to see if the class is full. The calculation includes an If statement:

```
If [sEnrollmentCount ≥ MaxClassSize]
```

If the statement is true (the class is full), the result of the calculation is the text *Class Full* shown in red.

Figure 2.8 shows the full text of the calculation as shown in the window where it is created.

The variable warning is set to the result of this calculation. But you can do more: Create a series of variables called warning1, warning2, and so forth. Each uses the same logic to test for some potential problem. A final variable, anyWarning, simply concatenates all of warnings together. If you display anyWarning in a layout, you see all of the potential problems with the data. To check if there are no problems, just check that the length of anyWarning is 0.

As you will see in Chapter 3, you can automatically perform error checking for variables in FileMaker. However, this approach enables you to perform the error checking and store the data while preserving the warnings for action at a future time.

If you are not familiar with the use of the calculation window, review the online help and documentation that are provided with FileMaker. You will use this window repeatedly in the projects that follow.

FIGURE 2.8 **Create an expression for a calculation field.**

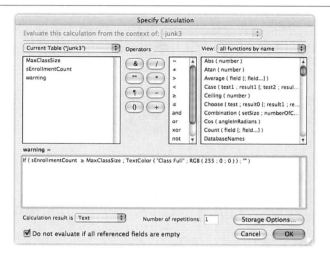

Developing a Runtime (Standalone) Solution

In this chapter you have seen some of the features you can use in FileMaker in a noninteractive way. Before moving on, it is important to note that you can create an interactive FileMaker solution that does not require people to use FileMaker itself. If you have FileMaker Advanced, choose Developer Utilities from the Tools menu to open the window shown in Figure 2.9.

FIGURE 2.9 **Create stand-alone solutions with FileMaker Advanced.**

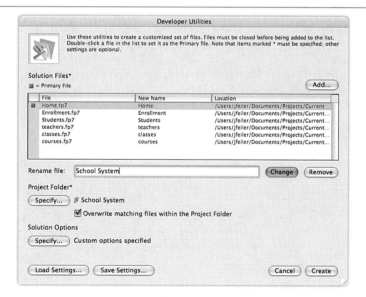

You add all of the FileMaker files for your solution using the Add button. One of the files must be marked as the primary file—click next to it to place the red dot next to the primary file. (Note that all files must be closed during this process.)

You can set a variety of options as shown in Figure 2.10.

FIGURE 2.10   Set solution options.

Standalone solutions are limited in that they are truly standalone: You cannot network standalone solutions in the ways that you can when people are using FileMaker itself. With that limitation, you can turn almost any of the projects described in Part II into standalone solutions.

PART II: Projects

CHAPTER 3: Building FileMaker Solutions

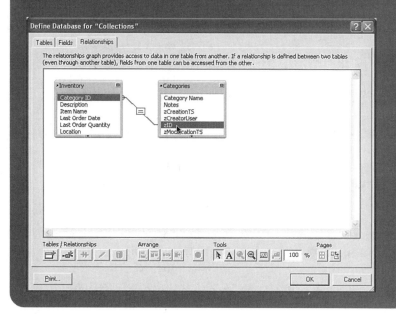

About the Project

This project provides an introduction to building all of the projects that you will build with FileMaker. In addition to the basics, it provides you with optional steps you can use to share the database over a network and to import data from a spreadsheet.

Prerequisites

Chapter 1, "Hands-On with FileMaker," provided an overview of interactive use of FileMaker; Chapter 2, "Automating FileMaker," continued on with an overview of the scripting and other tools you can use to create a FileMaker solution in which many of the actions are performed behind the scenes. These chapters build on the documentation that comes with FileMaker both in the online help and the documents that you can find installed with FileMaker (usually in the English Extras folder).

@work resources

Please visit the publisher's website to access the following Chapter 3 files:

▶ File4Normalized.fp7

Planning a FileMaker Solution

Now it is time to look at projects you can create with FileMaker. This chapter provides you not only with project design tips and techniques but also with the database architecture planning that you need to know in order to make your FileMaker solutions as productive as possible.

Each of the projects in this part provides a real-life example that you can use as-is or modify. Each project has been chosen to demonstrate particular features of FileMaker as well as to address a variety of business needs. You will find that the projects in each chapter are almost complete. The "almost" is because planning a FileMaker solution almost always starts with the same basic steps. In this chapter, you will see how to plan a FileMaker solution. These steps are not repeated in the later chapters except in the cases where you might need to vary the basic planning steps. You start by answering some basic questions to plan your FileMaker solution; having done that, it is time to start actually implementing your solution. After that, some specific issues with regard to layouts and databases need your attention.

FileMaker is a remarkably powerful tool that can be used easily for projects large and small. One of the greatest features of FileMaker is the ease with which you can make changes as a project evolves. Your needs might change; also, as you start working with a FileMaker solution, you and your colleagues might realize that you can ask new questions and get even more useful

answers. In traditional project development processes, such changes in midstream are expensive and often not even possible. With FileMaker, you can start with a simple project and let it evolve over time.

However, taking some time at the start to plan the project is time well spent. The most important difference between this type of planning with FileMaker and up-front planning on traditional IT projects is that the stakes are much lower with FileMaker. Make your best guesses as to the answers to these questions, knowing that changes will not be the end of the world.

What Is the Scope of the Project?

You can do so much with FileMaker that it can be tempting to start out trying to accomplish too much. Specify the scope of the project, bearing in mind that whether you work in a large corporation or in a part-time business of your own, it is better to get a basic system up and running quickly rather than to fiddle around for months (or years) trying to develop the ultimate system.

What Information Do You Need to Handle?

If you're working in a business you know, this might be the most difficult question to answer. You are probably so close to the data that it is hard to separate the wheat from the chaff. Make a list of the data you need to manage. Do not worry if it is incomplete (or too complete)—you can easily change it with FileMaker. But at least start with a list of your data.

How Should You Talk About the Data?

Every business has its own lingo. Often, people make fun of computer-ese, but, in fact, computer-ese pales next to the jargon of lawyers, librarians, and just about everyone else who works in a specific business. In designing your FileMaker solution, use the language of your users. If you are your own user, this is easy. Resist the temptation to show off your database skills—do not make people learn a new language in order to use your solution.

What Are the Rules Governing the Data?

Every time you can establish a rule for the data you deal with, you can translate that rule into a validation routine that FileMaker can automatically perform. For each rule you need to ask yourself (or whoever will use the system), "Is this always true?" Can you *ever* have two customers with the same name? Will the sale price to the customer *always* be greater than your acquisition cost? Even during a special sale? If the answer is "sometimes," that does not mean the rule is invalid—it just means that you have to accommodate exceptions in FileMaker's validation routines.

The more rules you can devise, the cleaner your data will be. But do not become sidetracked with rules for data that is rarely used. If the place cards for the fiftieth anniversary party of the business have a special rule for their data, that is nice; but get on with the rules for day-to-day operations.

What Reports Do You Need?

If you are automating an existing system, you already have some reports to use as a model. Do you want to replicate them? Or is this an opportunity to start from scratch? Do you need paper reports or a paper trail, or will onscreen reports be sufficient? Are there specific paper sizes and forms with which you need to work? Know this up front so you can design layouts once.

> ### ✎ NOTE
> If you are dealing with preprinted forms or multipart forms, check to see if you can make changes. It is much easier to print a report twice (or more often) than to print it on two- or multipart paper. Likewise, aligning your FileMaker data with preprinted forms can be tedious; if it is necessary, do it, but it is worth asking whether the special forms are necessary.

Do You Need to Import or Export Data?

This is an important question. Are you going to be converting data or starting from scratch with your new FileMaker solution?

Do You Have Ongoing Import/Export Needs?

If your solution is to be part of a larger system, you might need to move data into and out of it. FileMaker handles importing and exporting of data, but you should know from the start if you are going to have to do this. If you can avoid it for your first project, you will have an easier time.

What Are Your Security Needs?

Security is one of the three aspects of a project that is hard to add on after the fact. (The other two are networking and version control.) If you will be the only one using the solution and if you only use one computer that is under your control, you can skip this question. Otherwise, consider who will need access to the data. You might want to review the FileMaker security model to see what you can do. (A document on security is provided in the Electronic Documentation folder inside the English Extras folder when you install FileMaker.)

Implementing a FileMaker Solution

After you've done your planning (or as much of it as you feel comfortable doing), it is time to start implementing your solution. This section walks you through the basics of implementing a solution. Many steps are involved, but most of them are quite simple. You can come back and change your mind in almost every case, so there is no reason not to get started.

Project: Setting Up Your First Database

We'll be setting up a database in eight easy steps:

STEPS ▼

1. **Getting started**
2. **Creating tables**
3. **Creating fields**
4. **Creating relationships**
5. **Creating a layout**
6. **Testing your solution**
7. **Sharing FileMaker databases on a network**
8. **Converting and normalizing a spreadsheet**

STEP 1 ▼
Getting Started

To begin, choose New Database from the File menu. Give it a name that makes sense.

📌 **TIP**

You might have several versions of your solution as you develop it. You might want to save a copy of the solution in a safe place while you experiment with new features so you can go back to the saved version if necessary. Do not rename the solution. Instead, create folders (or directories) reflecting the stages of development. To save a copy of the entire solution, just copy the folder that it is in and rename the folder—something like "Wednesday OK Version" or "Before Data Entry." Inside the folder, you can include not only the database but also any relevant documents, data in a spreadsheet or text file that you might need to run in to the database, graphics for your layouts, and so forth. To be even safer, zip these folders and remove the originals. That way, you will not accidentally open an old database file in a folder that has been copied.

Each of the projects in Part II has its own database requirements, so you need to know your way around the basics of the Define

Database dialog (accessible from the File menu). It opens as soon as you have named your database.

A FileMaker database (starting with FileMaker 7) can contain a number of database tables. As with other *relational database managers*, FileMaker stores its data in tables that have rows and columns (sometimes called records and fields). A FileMaker database file can contain all of your solution's tables or none of them. In addition to tables, a database file contains scripts, layouts, and security controls. These can apply to and be used by any of the tables in the database file. In addition, you can share database files and their tables.

STEP 2 ▼
Creating Tables

By default, a single table is created in your new database file. Its name is the name of the database file. You can delete this table or rename it if you want to create a table with another name. The database file used in the first three chapters of this book contains two tables, shown in Figure 3.1. (The figures in this section show FileMaker Advanced. The buttons that enable you to copy, paste, and import tables are not available in FileMaker Pro.)

FIGURE 3.1   Create tables in the Define Database dialog.

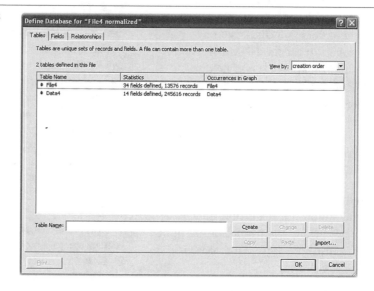

STEP 3 ▼
Creating Fields

To start creating fields, click the Fields tab in the Define Database dialog and select the table in which you want to create fields from the drop-down menu at the upper left of the window. Each field should have a meaningful name, and if there is any ambiguity, add a comment to the field name at the bottom of the window. Figure 3.2 shows the Fields tab in the Define Database dialog.

FIGURE 3.2   Define fields
in your table.

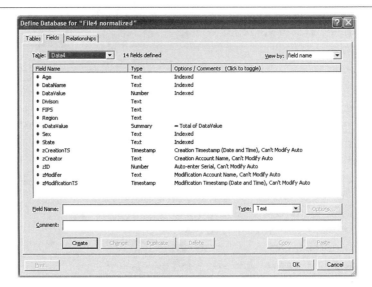

Choose the type of field you want to use. A good rule of thumb is to choose the most specific type of field you can. If you are storing numbers in a field, FileMaker is able to convert the contents of a text field to numbers as needed, but you can't apply numeric formatting to the text field. In order to use numeric formatting (as well as numeric validation for data entry), define numeric fields as numeric. Likewise, define dates as dates and times as times.

As shown in Figure 3.3, you can switch between the options for fields and their comments by clicking the header of the right column. You also can change the order in which fields are shown.

You will see how to use the types of fields in the later projects.

 TIP

Keep your data pure! Do not use special values for special meaning. 999 is a number—it does not represent missing data. –1 is a number—it should not be used to mean not applicable. Billions of dollars were spent rewriting software before the year 2000 in large part because certain values (such as the two-digit years 99 and 00) were used for special meanings. FileMaker has built into it a missing value: blank. You can test for it by testing the length of the contents of a field (if you test for its numeric value, a blank has the same value as zero, but its length is zero while the length of a numeric zero is one character).

If you absolutely must have descriptive information, consider using a pair of fields. One field can contain a data value, and the other can contain information about the value such as actual, estimated, and the like.

STEP 4 ▼
Creating Relationships

Each table you have created is shown in the Relationships tab of the Define Database dialog, as you can see in Figure 3.4.

FIGURE 3.3   Add
comments to field names
where appropriate.

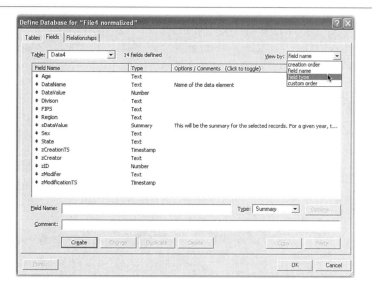

FIGURE 3.4   Use the
Relationships tab to manage
tables in your database.

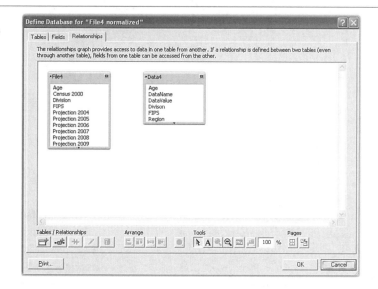

Relationships are defined to link records in one table with records in another table; they are drawn as lines on the *relationship graph* shown in Figure 3.5. One of the most frequent reasons to do this is if the number of records in one table for a given entity differs from the number in another table. For example, you might have a table containing categories of items in a collection. Each category can have several inventory items associated with it. If you try to squeeze all of the inventory information into the categories table (perhaps as item1, item2, and so forth), you will encounter problems. Instead, the preferred method is to assign a unique ID to each category and to use it as the related field for a table containing inventory items. Each inventory item has a `Category ID` field that is related to the `zID` field in the `category` table. (The use of the name `zID` for ID fields is common; because the field is used internally, it is prefixed with *z* so it appears at the bottom of alphabetized field listings, below the more visible fields such as `name`, `price`, `address`, and so forth.)

By using this relationship, you are able to get from any given inventory item to the related category information (`Category Name`, for example). Relationships go in the other direction, too. From a given category you can get to that category's inventory items. This is precisely the situation that will be explored in the Collections Database project in Chapter 5, "Managing One-to-Many Relationships." Figure 3.5 shows its relationship graph; as you can see, in addition to the tables in the relationship graph, there are now lines indicating the relationship.

FIGURE 3.5 **Lines indicate relationships.**

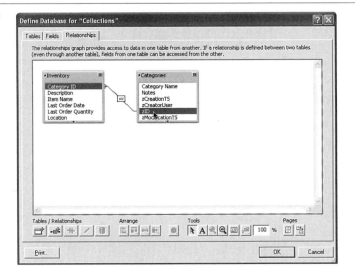

This structure can be replicated in many levels. For example, a category may have many inventory items, and an inventory item may belong to many categories. To implement this, you might have three tables that are related to one another:

▶ `zID` in the `Inventory` table is related to `Category ID` in the `Categories` table as shown in Figure 3.5.

▶ `ID` in the `Categories` table is related to `Inventory ID` in a new table called `InventoriesAndCategories`. This

structure allows you to have many categories assigned to a single inventory item and many inventory items assigned to a category. This type of relationship is called a *many-to-many relationship*; it is the basis of the Boutique Manager project in Chapter 6, "Managing Many-to-Many Relationships."

As you will see, you implement these relationships by drawing lines from one table to another. Relationships can be quite complex; they need not be equal. You can have a relationship of all orders with balances over a certain amount; you can use dates as the basis of relationships. The projects in this book show a wide variety of relationships.

The process of organizing data into a set of related database tables is called *normalization*. Rules are available that can guide you through the process, but as you will see later, you can be guided just as easily by common sense and by making certain that your data is not duplicated. (The process of normalizing a spreadsheet is described in the "Converting and Normalizing a Spreadsheet" section later in this chapter.)

For now, you just need to know that you can create tables, fields, and relationships with the Define Database dialog and that you will use it in each of the projects of in this book.

STEP 5 ▼
Creating a Layout

Your first layout needs to have data entry fields for the fields in your table. It is not hard to create the layout: FileMaker will do it by default. As soon as you have finished entering the names of your fields into the Define Database dialog, you will have a layout you can use to enter and display data.

STEP 6 ▼
Testing your Solution

At every step of the development process, test your solution. Test it to see that it does what you want it to do. Then go back and test it to

see if it fails properly. This is one of the most common problems: Your solution works right if you enter the right data, but sometimes you (or someone else) enter something that is wrong. Do you accommodate human frailty and data errors?

One tip for testing any software is to have someone else do the testing (just as you have someone else proofread what you have written).

STEP 7 ▼
Sharing FileMaker Databases on a Network

Along with security, it is hard to retrofit networking and data sharing after you have designed a solution (this applies to any software, not just FileMaker solutions). If you are certain that your data will never be shared, you do not have to worry about networking. However, it is safest to consider the possibility of networking and data sharing so that, even if you do not need it now, you can use it in the future.

Three ways of sharing FileMaker databases on networks are

- ▶ FileMaker sharing
- ▶ FileMaker Server
- ▶ Web sharing

Using FileMaker Sharing

If you have a network, you can share FileMaker databases over it. You can turn on sharing from one copy of FileMaker and connect to it from another copy of FileMaker on that network. Because you can locate FileMaker by using a network IP address, this sharing can even happen over the Internet, provided that you know the IP address of the computer on which FileMaker is running.

In order to connect to a shared database, use the Open Remote command from the File menu; you will see the copies of FileMaker that are sharing databases on your local network. You can also type in the IP address of a FileMaker computer that is not on your network.

This type of sharing is appropriate for a small number of users; the software limits that number to five.

Using FileMaker Server

For more than five users, you need to use FileMaker Server. This is software that runs on a computer (it need not be a specific server computer, but that is often preferred), and it does nothing except share FileMaker databases. It manages users, can control backups, and enables you to open and close databases. However, FileMaker Server does not enable you to create or edit databases as FileMaker Pro does.

FileMaker Server has no visible interface; you use FileMaker Server Admin to manage the FileMaker Server software. It is often desirable to install FileMaker Server Admin on one or more computers on a network other than the computer where FileMaker Server itself is running. That gives you access to FileMaker Server itself without needing to physically touch the server computer which might be locked away in a secure location.

Using the Web

You can share databases using Web technology. FileMaker supports Instant Web Publishing that puts your databases on the Web so you can use a web browser to access the databases. With Instant Web Publishing, what you see in a browser is very close to what people see using FileMaker itself as a client.

You can exert additional control over your web databases by using Custom Web Publishing with FileMaker Server Advanced, which relies on XML/XSLT, two industry-wide standards for web publication. Instant Web Publishing is discussed in Chapter 11, "Implementing a Simple Web Publishing Solution"; Custom Web Publishing is not.

STEP 8 ▼
Converting and Normalizing a Spreadsheet

Here is a taste of a very small project that can get you started using the tools described in the three chapters of this part of the book. The process of building tables and relationships that is summarized here is explored in detail in the next three chapters.

Convert the Spreadsheet to FileMaker

As described in Chapter 1, a spreadsheet can be downloaded from the U.S. Census Bureau website; it contains population estimates through 2030 by age and sex for each state. It also contains 2000 actual population numbers by state for each age and sex.

To convert it to a FileMaker database, you can simply drag it onto the FileMaker icon. What you get is a database that contains the spreadsheet data. It looks like a spreadsheet, and, in Table view, it behaves like a spreadsheet.

Rename the Fields

In fact, the table that is created in this way is table `File4` of the file `File4 normalized.fp7` that is available on this book's website. There is only one difference between table `File4` and the table that is generated by the automatic conversion: The field names in the automatic conversion are named `Field 1`, `Field 2`, and so forth.

Open the Define Database dialog and change the names of the fields to more meaningful names. You can tell what they should be because the first few records of the converted file have headings that describe the columns. `File4 normalized.fp7` has renamed fields in it. These are names such as `Age`, `Census 2000`, `Projection 2004`, `Projection 2005`, `Region`, `Sex`, and `State`.

Eliminate Unneeded Data

This step starts to clean up the data. Some blank lines are in the spreadsheet. In addition, there are totals. Those can be calculated easily by FileMaker. Using Find mode, find lines where `Age` is `blank` or contains the string `Total`. Delete these found records.

Naming Conventions

FileMaker warns you about certain naming conventions. Characters such as +, <, or spaces make field names hard to use in calculations. Field names beginning with numbers or containing spaces might create problems, particularly when you are using them with the Web.

These are matters of judgment, and you should be guided by the purpose of your database. If you know that your database will be published on the Web, avoid internal spaces within names as well as any special characters, even if FileMaker allows them.

In addition to making names meaningful, there are some commonly used conventions. These help to group fields together in alphabetized listings. Here are some of the common conventions. They all relate to the initial character used in a name:

▶ g—These are global fields.

▶ c—These are calculations.

▶ z—These are internally used fields such as serial numbers (commonly called `zID`), modification timestamps, and the like.

▶ s—These are summary fields.

Normalize the Data

If you start to manipulate the data, you will see that it is awkward to work with the string of fields for each projected year. A lot of repeating data is in the database. Normalizing it as much as possible makes it easier to work with. Instead of putting all of the projections for a state, age, and sex together in one record, you can split up the record. Figure 3.4, shown previously in this chapter, shows the fields of a new table, `Data4`, that are normalized.

It is worth looking at each of these fields so you understand how normalization works.

The idea is that each data element is a separate record. Thus, each record needs to be identified by the Age, Sex, and State fields. Another field, DataName, is used to indicate the year of the projection. Together, these four fields uniquely identify every number on the spreadsheet. (The table Data4 also contains some census identification—FIPS, Division, and Region—that are not needed in the example but have been preserved in the database.) In addition to the fields that identify a data value, you need the value itself—DataValue. This field is a numeric field, not a text field.

The last important field is a summary field, sDataValue. It is a summary that represents the total of all DataValue fields currently displayed. If you experiment with the database, you will see that selecting the records where DataValue contains the string 2000 gives you all of the actual 2000 census records, and the sDataValue field displays the total population of the United States according to the 2000 census.

Finally, there are five fields that many FileMaker database designers automatically add to every database table: Their names start with z (so they appear at the bottom of an alphabetized field list), and they contain timestamp and other information about the record. They can help with debugging. Throughout this book these are referred to as administrative fields, and they appear in almost every table. All are auto-entered by FileMaker, and the option is set to prevent modification by users. As a result, you can rely on these fields containing accurate data:

- ▶ **zID**—Unique serial number generated by FileMaker

- ▶ **zCreator**—User or FileMaker account name of the creator of the record

- ▶ **zCreationTS**—Timestamp of creation

- ▶ **zModifer**—User or FileMaker account name of the previous modifier

- ▶ **zModificationTS**—Timestamp of previous modification

After you have the Data4 table created with these fields, you now need to create scripts to normalize the data. The scripts that do this were described in the preceding chapter, and they are provided in the file that you download from the website. You can now go back and see what happens as a long, unnormalized record containing projections for 2004 to 2030 is split into its component data values.

Make a copy of File4 normalized.fp7, and go to the layout that displays Data4 (the new table). From the Records menu, select Show All Records, and then, from the same menu, choose Delete All Records. Data4 is now empty, and you can run the script to convert all of the data. It takes a few minutes (but not many), and all the data is converted.

Experiment in finding all the data for a certain year, state, or sex. Look at the sDataValue display: If the numbers are strange, look for extraneous records. (For example, if they are too big, you have left fields with the total number of records in the database.)

This part of the book has reviewed the basics of FileMaker that you need for the later projects. You might need to look at some of the documentation again or explore the online help if you are uncertain about some areas. If you can work your way through the normalization process described in this section, you are ready to move on to the rest of the projects.

CHAPTER 4: Managing Inventory

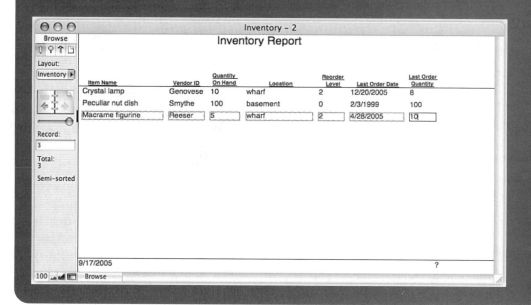

About the Project

This project is a template for keeping track of similar items—people, assets, real estate, parts, and so forth. In addition, this chapter provides you with a good introduction to various FileMaker layout and data entry tools.

Prerequisites

Before you start to build this or any other database, you should know the basics of using FileMaker to enter and retrieve data. You should be comfortable with the terminology and concepts that are covered in the first three chapters. You need FileMaker Pro to complete this project. Although the examples in this book have been built with FileMaker 8, you can use FileMaker 7 in most cases.

@work resources

Please visit the publisher's website to access the following Chapter 4 files:

▶ Inventory.fp7

Planning the Project

Begin by reviewing Chapter 3, "Building FileMaker Solutions." Then, consider issues specific to the inventory project.

What Are You Keeping Track Of?

This project enables you to keep track of similar objects: students, furniture, and so forth. If you need to keep track of objects that can be contained within other objects or that can be combined, you have a more complex data model to handle. Chapter 5, "Managing One-to-Many Relationships," and Chapter 6, "Managing Many-to-Many Relationships," address such data models.

What Information Will You Store?

The information you store guides you as you set up the fields in the database. Note that this step, which is critical to the success of any project, needs to be done before you actually begin to build the database. With FileMaker, it is easy to add and modify fields as you go along, but the more you have planned at the beginning, the easier your task will be.

As you plan the data that you store, do a reality check for each field. Write down some examples of the data that you will store.

 TIP

In this project, you have four fields to identify and describe the items that you are storing. Resist the temptation to bring manual processes into the database. Good database design requires that each field have one item of information in it. If you want to identify an item by a code that combines location, item name, and vendor ID, do not do so: You have separate fields for those data elements (and you can create more). You can always combine database fields on layouts and reports, but you cannot always split them apart.

For this project, the data that you track consists of

- ▶ **Item Name**—This is the name that appears on reports. It should be a fairly short name that is easily recognized by users of the system. Note that the identification of each item relies on this field as well as the following three fields.

- ▶ **Description**—This is description of the item. It can be longer than the item name, which means that you can provide more details.

- ▶ **Vendor ID**—This is a code that you can use in ordering the item from a vendor. This might or might not uniquely identify the item (if you deal with multiple vendors and each uses its own identification numbers, the Vendor ID field might have duplicate identifiers in it).

- ▶ **zID**—This is a *unique identifier* for each record in your table. It is automatically generated by FileMaker. The field name begins with *z* so it is at the bottom in an alphabetical listing of fields, along with other internally used fields you create.

- ▶ **Quantity On Hand**—This is the heart of the inventory system—how many you have.

- ▶ **Location**—You might want to indicate where the items are located. If the items are students, for example, keep track of what grade they are in; if items are inventory items, know which warehouse they are in.

- ▶ **Reorder Level**—For items where a supply is required, you can keep track of the inventory level at which you need to re-order.

- ▶ **Last Order Date**—This database enables you to track the last order. This field tells you when that order took place.

- ▶ **Last Order Quantity**—This field tells you how many items you ordered last time. Together with Last Order Date and Quantity On Hand, you can make an informed guess as to the number you should order next time.

- ▶ **zCreator, zCreationTS, zModifier, zModificationTS**—These fields are automatically filled in by FileMaker and keep track of who created or modified the record, as well as the time-stamps of creation and modification.

These are the fields used in this project. When you build your own inventory system, you might come up with another set of fields. If you are keeping track of employees, the Quantity On Hand and Last Order fields are obviously irrelevant. On the other hand, if you are keeping track of order information, you might need to track the vendor from whom you purchased the item. You should settle on the basic fields when you plan your project even though you can modify them later.

 TIP

You should do your database planning first. The first time you work through this project (or any other project in this book), however, you might want to limit your modifications so the project you build is close to (if not identical to) the project in the book. After you have duplicated the book's project, it is easy to go back, plan your own, and implement it.

How Many Items Are There to Keep Track Of?

This piece of information is important in designing the user interface. If a dozen items are to be inventoried, they can be identified in a drop-down menu or by radio buttons. If there are a thousand items, you will need another type of interface.

What Are the Rules and Characteristics of the Data?

Can items have duplicate names? Do items have identification numbers supplied by vendors? Are these consistent numbers or does each vendor have its own identifiers for items that are otherwise identical? This background information helps you make the right decisions when you implement rules for data entry and *validation*.

Project:
Inventory Manager

We'll be creating the Inventory database solution in six easy steps:

STEPS ▼
1. **Getting started**
2. **Setting up a one-table database**
3. **Setting auto-entries for fields**
4. **Implementing the data rules for validation**
5. **Creating your first layout**
6. **Creating the report**

STEP 1 ▼
Getting Started

Start by launching FileMaker Pro. (You can use FileMaker Pro Advanced, but for this project, either one will work.) If you see the dialog that prompts you to open an existing file or create a new one, choose to create a new one, as shown in Figure 4.1. If there is no dialog visible, use the New Database command from the File menu.

FIGURE 4.1   **Create a new empty database.**

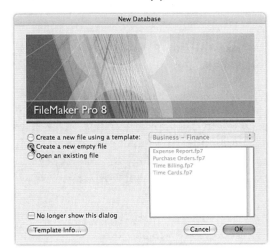

STEP 2 ▼
Setting Up a One-Table Database

You are prompted to name your database file. This file will contain only a single table. When you name a new database file, that name is used to automatically create the first table in the file. Although you can rename the file and the table within it, it is easier to name the database file Inventory and allow FileMaker to create a single table within it that is also called Inventory.

FileMaker opens a window containing a blank layout based on the default table it has created; in front of that window, the Define Database dialog appears, ready for you to enter the database *schema* (see Figure 4.2).

FIGURE 4.2 **FIGURE 4.2** **The Define Database dialog enables you to build your database schema.**

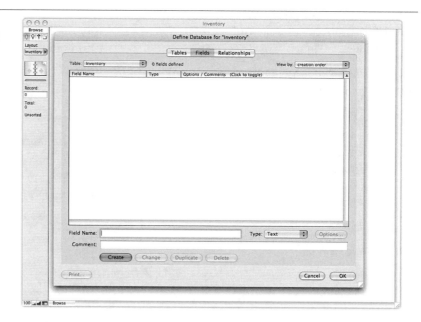

At this point, you can proceed in two general ways. You can create each of your database fields, return to the fields to set the auto-entry options with auto-entries, and return again to set validation rules for data entry. Alternatively, you can use the Options button to open the Options dialog as soon as you have created each field. You can proceed in either manner, or you can mix and match as long as you get the work done. For the sake of clarity, this project describes creating all the fields first, then setting the auto-entry options, and finally setting data entry validations. Whether you follow that pattern or the alternate pattern is up to you.

Create the database fields. In the "Planning the Project" section, the database fields were described. All you need to do now is to create them in the Define Database dialog. Note that the names provided here include spaces; if you are going to be using XDBC or publishing the database on the Web,

including spaces can pose problems. But for this database, those are not issues about which to be concerned.

Note, too, that when you create the fields, you need to assign a type to each field. The database works properly if you leave each field as the default type—text. FileMaker handles conversions as necessary. If you use the most precise type possible, however, it helps with error-checking and formatting. All of the database fields are of type Text except the following:

- ▶ zID is a number.
- ▶ zCreationTS is a timestamp.
- ▶ zModificationTS is a timestamp.
- ▶ Quantity On Hand is a number.
- ▶ Reorder Level is a number.
- ▶ Last Order Date is a date.
- ▶ Last Order Quantity is a number.

When you have finished entering the fields, the Define Database dialog displays them all, as shown in Figure 4.3.

If your Define Database dialog does not look like this, two possible explanations are

▸ This dialog shows the complete database schema. The right column (Options / Comments) might look different. That could be because it is showing the comments, not the

options. In that case, simply click the column title to switch back to options. Also note that the options shown in Figure 4.3 have been set already. They are set in steps 3 and 4 in this project, but, as noted previously, can be set as you create each field.

▸ If the sequence of fields is different in your Database Design dialog, use the drop-down menu in the upper right of the dialog to change the order.

FIGURE 4.3 **The Define Database dialog shows all the fields.**

STEP 3 ▼
Setting Auto-Entries for Fields

Any time you can automatically enter data in a field, you avoid one of the most common sources of data entry error: operator errors. If you ask people to enter data that can be automatically entered, you might annoy or tire them. A few moments thinking about what values can be automatically entered pays off in efficiency for your solution and improved data accuracy. Note that auto-entered data need not be permanent. You can automatically enter data that is likely to be correct and allow the user to change it.

The five fields starting with z all have auto-entry options set. These fields are used in many databases, often with the same names. Because you can ask FileMaker to fill in the data, there is no burden on users when you implement these fields, and you will have built a powerful audit trail for your database.

Figure 4.4 shows the Auto-Enter tab of the Options dialog.

Note the check box at the bottom of Figure 4.4. By preventing people from modifying the auto-enter values, you can rely on the values. In particular, a serial number, on whose uniqueness you depend, should not be modifiable.

FIGURE 4.4   Use auto-enter options where possible to speed and improve data entry.

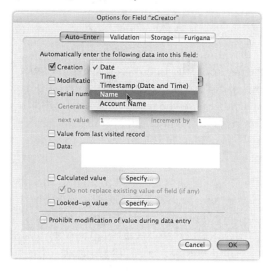

You can choose to use the user name or FileMaker account name for the creator or modifier of the record. In many cases, these are the same. But if you use a shared account name (such as the default, admin), specify the user name. Alternatively, if your environment has computers that are shared, the user names might not be reliable and the account names are safer to use. In a worst-case scenario, you can create fields for both account name and user name. With FileMaker filling in the data, this does not slow down the system.

STEP 4 ▼
Implementing the Data Rules for Validation

In planning the project, you have already decided on data validation rules. Remember that the more you validate the data on data entry, the more reliable it is. You set validation rules in the Validation tab of the Options dialog. In this project, two validation rules are implemented:

▶ Item Name is required to be non-blank, as shown in Figure 4.5. This rule also implements a custom message. This rule is necessary only so users can understand reports and layouts. Internally, items are identified by their unique serial number (zID), which users never see. Items can have blank names as far as the FileMaker database is concerned, but that would be inconvenient for users.

▶ Vendor ID is also required. However, the validation rule allows the user to override this edit during data entry. This means that you can have a blank Vendor ID field, and you must not rely on it being present. (The reason why an edit for a field such as this may be overridden is that the user might not have the information when the data is being entered. Do you want to stop data entry while the user looks up the vendor's ID number for an item or do you want to continue and allow it to be entered later? Or—horrors—do you want to force the user to enter a fake number that will sooner or later cause a problem when people forget that it was a fake placeholder?)

FIGURE 4.5   Set validation options.

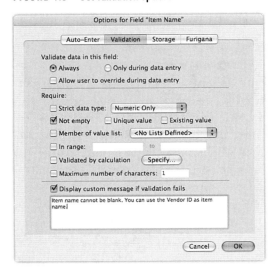

STEP 5 ▼
Creating Your First Layout

This is the easiest step of all. When you have finished creating your fields and setting the options for auto-entry and validation, click OK to close the Database Design dialog. The blank layout that appeared behind it when you created the database now contains all of your fields, as shown in Figure 4.6.

FIGURE 4.6   FileMaker builds a layout for you.

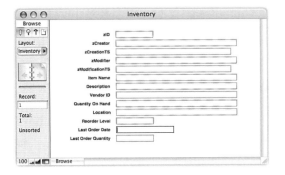

FileMaker uses the settings for fonts and sizes that you have in place before you create the database. The fields are shown in the order in which you created them. You can rearrange them and change their styles as you want. But if you do not want to bother with that, you will always have a layout you can use to enter and display data as soon as you have created a database.

STEP 6 ▼
Creating the Report

Although you can make do with the default layouts, it is easy to create your own layouts with FileMaker. One way is to use the New Layout/Report assistant as described in this section. (Other projects use different techniques to create layouts). Go into Layout mode either by choosing Layout mode from the View menu or by clicking the Layout icon at the top of the status area; proceed by choosing New Layout/Report from the Layouts menu as shown in Figure 4.7.

Each layout is based on a given table. By default, it is the table you are working with (Inventory, in this case), from which you show records. You can show records from other tables, but there is only one base table for each layout. FileMaker gives a default name—the name of the base table—to the layout. If you follow the steps in this project exactly, you create a layout in this step named Inventory. That is the same name as the default layout that was created in the previous step. Nothing prevents you from having duplicate layout names, but it is useful not to do so, and you might want to change one or both of these layout names using the Layout Setup command.

FIGURE 4.7   **Create a new layout.**

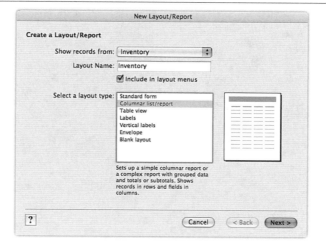

For this report, select the Columnar List/Report option as shown in Figure 4.7.

The next panel, shown in Figure 4.8, enables you to choose whether the report should be displayed with grouped data. In this case, ungrouped data (the first radio button) is the correct choice.

On the next panel, shown in Figure 4.9, you specify the fields for the report. In this case, all of the fields in the table are used except

- ▶ There is no need to display the internal fields (the names that start with z).

- ▶ The item description, designed as a lengthier field than the item name, is omitted from this report because of space.

The next panel, shown in Figure 4.10, enables you to sort the report. In this case, it is alphabetized by item name.

The next three panels enable you to control the overall appearance of the report. First, as shown in Figure 4.11, you select the theme for the report.

FIGURE 4.8 **Choose the columnar list/report layout.**

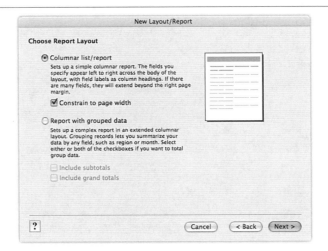

FIGURE 4.9 **Select the report's fields.**

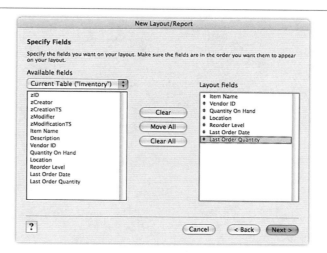

FIGURE 4.10 **Alphabetize the report.**

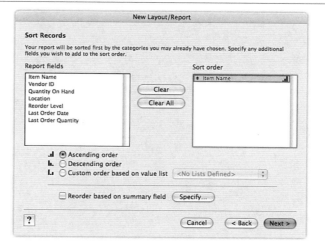

In Figure 4.12, you can select the title, page number, and other identifying information for the header and footer of the report. Note that page numbers are only displayed properly when you view the report in Preview mode.

FIGURE 4.11   Select the
report's theme.

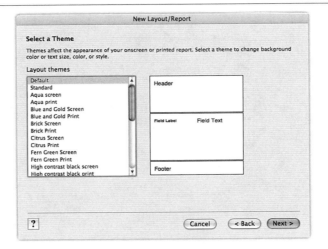

FIGURE 4.12   Set the
report header and footer.

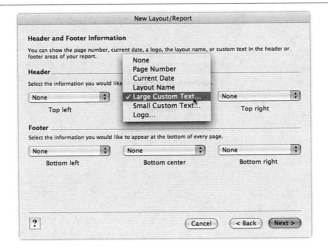

If you have custom text in the header or
footer, you are prompted to enter it as shown
in Figure 4.13.

Just two steps are left. You can choose if you
want a script to be created for the report; if
you choose this option, you can name it as
shown in Figure 4.14. It is a good idea to
have a script created automatically, particularly if your report relies on sorted data. That
way FileMaker builds the script with the
correct sort for you.

FIGURE 4.13   Enter custom text for the report title.

The final panel confirms the entire process. You can choose to continue in Preview mode, looking at the report, or you can go into Layout mode to make your own customizations. Figure 4.15 shows the final panel.

If you followed these steps, the script shown in Figure 4.16 has been created for you.

Go into Layout mode to tweak the layout created for you by FileMaker, as shown in Figure 4.17.

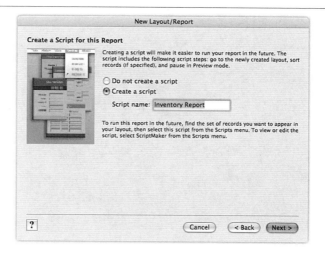

FIGURE 4.14 **Allow FileMaker to create a script to sort the data for the report.**

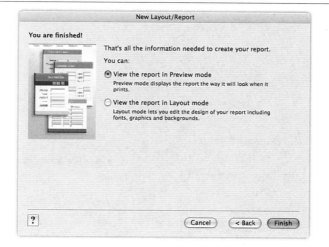

FIGURE 4.15 **Complete the layout and go into Preview or Layout mode.**

FIGURE 4.16 **FileMaker creates the script to sort the data and run the report.**

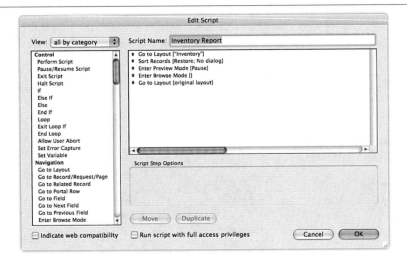

FIGURE 4.17 **The layout FileMaker created takes up two lines.**

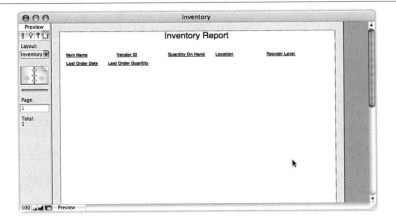

Because you know the data with which you are dealing, you can rearrange fields and titles so all of the data for a single record is shown on a single line. When you are finished, FileMaker might ask you if you want to confirm the layout changes with the dialog shown in Figure 4.18. (Note that you can turn off this dialog in the future with the check box.)

FIGURE 4.18 **Confirm your layout changes (and, if you want, stop FileMaker from asking you about changes in the future).**

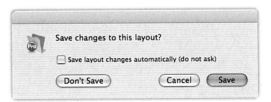

This layout and the associated script can be used to produce an alphabetized inventory list. You can also use it in Browse mode, as shown in Figure 4.19, to enter data. If you use it for data entry, note that the page number in the lower-right corner is shown as a question mark—page numbers are calculated only when you go into Preview mode.

FIGURE 4.19   Enter data in the revised layout.

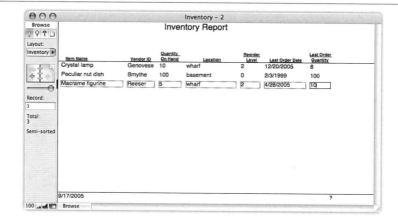

Final Thoughts

This project is very basic, both in its layout and in its database design. The steps you have gone through here are the basics for almost every FileMaker solution you will design. Even when you are quite proficient at creating your own layouts, you will often want to use the New Layout/Report assistant to provide you with a basis from which to work. Having FileMaker assemble the data and sort it (and group it, if you want to do that), enables you to concentrate on the customizations you need to do.

Now that the basics are done, it is time to move on to more complex projects.

CHAPTER 5: Managing One-to-Many Relationships

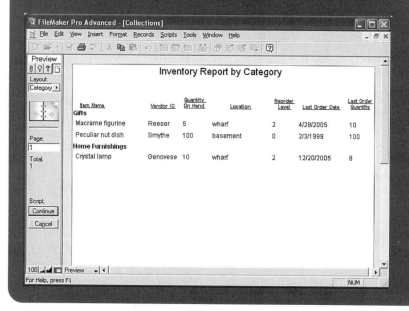

About the Project

This project builds on the previous project to help you organize things. In this project, the items you organize are grouped into collections. These could be museum collections of artifacts, classes of students, or any other groupings of objects or people. In this project, there is one primary constraint: An item can be in only one collection. This is called a one-to-many relationship. For many situations, this is a perfectly realistic limitation. At any given time, a student can be in only one class, and a fossil can be in only one display case. In other cases, however, this constraint is not realistic; those cases are handled in the following project.

Prerequisites

This project builds on the Inventory Manager project in Chapter 4, "Managing Inventory." You should understand that project before starting on this one.

@work resources

Please visit the publisher's website to access the following Chapter 5 files:

- ▶ Collections.fp7
- ▶ Shell.fp7

Planning the Project

Begin by reviewing Chapter 3, "Building FileMaker Solutions," as well as the planning issues from the previous project. Then, consider the groups you want to use. In some cases (students within classes, for example) the groups are obvious. In other cases, you need to give some thought to them. Remember that an item can be in only one collection at a time; also, collections cannot be inside other collections (both cases are handled in the next project, Chapter 6, "Managing Many-to-Many Relationships").

Project:
Collections Database

We'll be creating the Collections database solution in five easy steps:

STEPS ▼

1. **Getting started**
2. **Adding the Categories table**
3. **Relating the Categories table to the Inventory table**
4. **Creating the category report**
5. **Adding categories to data entry**

STEP 1 ▼
Getting Started

Begin by copying the Inventory database from the preceding chapter; rename the copied database Collections.

STEP 2 ▼
Adding the Categories Table

In this step, you add a second table to the database. The table contains the five administrative fields (the names of which start with z) along with a Category Name field and a Notes field.

> ### 📌 NOTE
>
> It is a good idea always to add a Notes field to each table. That enables the user to provide free-format notes and descriptions of the data in each record. This can help keep fields such as names and identifiers pure; comments such as "not for resale" or "broken" go into the Notes field, not into other fields where they do not belong.

You can create the table and manually enter those fields. However, if you frequently start every new table with those five fields, you can simplify your work if you are using FileMaker Pro Advanced. That method is described here.

Begin by creating a new database file called Shell. In its one table (by default also called Shell), create the five administrative fields just as you did in Chapter 4. Figure 5.1 shows the Define Database dialog with those fields created.

FIGURE 5.1   The Define
Database dialog enables you
to build your database
schema.

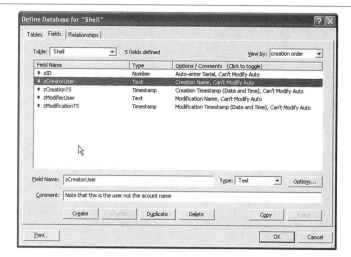

Now import this `Shell` table into the
Collections database.

> **NOTE**
>
> With FileMaker Pro Advanced, you can also copy and
> paste tables as you can see in Figure 5.1. For a single
> table, there is not a great deal of difference, but the
> Import command allows you to import several tables
> from one file at one time. This can be useful if you
> create a database file with a variety of standard tables
> that you use in many of your solutions.

Close the Shell database and open the
Collections database (this is the copy of
Inventory that you renamed). In the Define
Database dialog, click the Tables tab to see
the tables in the database. At this point there
is just one, the `Inventory` table that was
created in the preceding project. This is
shown in Figure 5.2.

Click the Import button in the lower right of
the dialog (remember that this feature is only
available in FileMaker Pro Advanced). You
are prompted to locate the file that contains
the table you want to import. When you
have identified the Shell database file, you
will see the dialog shown in Figure 5.3; it lists
all of the tables in that database file. Select
what you want to import. In this case, there
is only one table (`Shell`), and that is the
table you want to import.

The results of the import are shown, as you
can see in Figure 5.4.

As you can see from the text in the dialog,
FileMaker does a lot of error-checking during
import; it also might rename fields to avoid
duplication.

As you see when you dismiss the import
summary, you now have two tables in the
Collections database: `Inventory` and `Shell`
(see Figure 5.5).

FIGURE 5.2   The
Inventory **table is the only
table in the Collections database.**

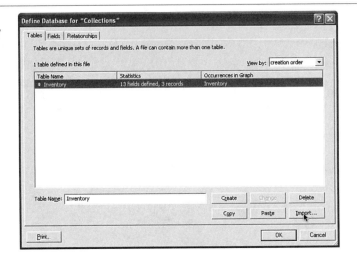

FIGURE 5.3   **Choose to
import the** Shell **table.**

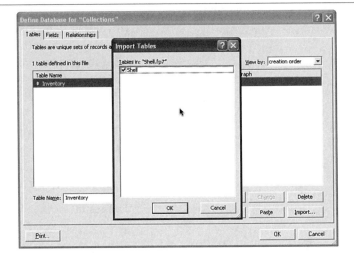

FIGURE 5.4   **FileMaker**
summarizes the results of
importing a table.

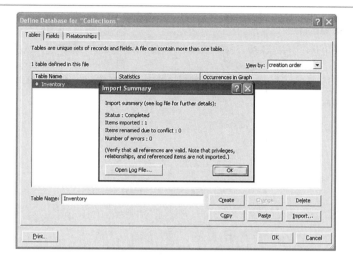

FIGURE 5.5   **The** Shell
table has been added to the
database file.

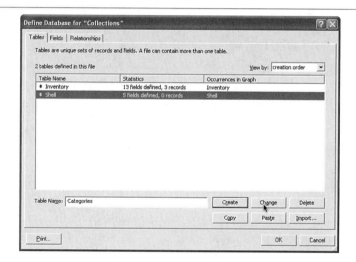

Complete the creation of the Categories table by changing the name of the Shell table to Categories (in the Tables tab of the Define Database dialog) and by adding Category Name and Notes (both text fields) in the Fields tab of the Define Database dialog. The finished Categories table is shown in Figure 5.6.

You can use the default layout to add records to the Categories table for testing.

FIGURE 5.6 Add fields
and change the table name
to complete this step.

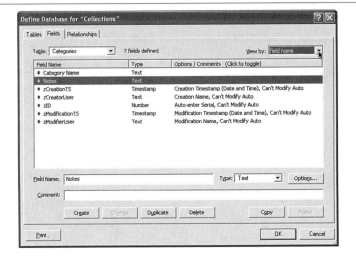

STEP 3 ▼
Relating the Categories Table to the Inventory Table

This is the step that unleashes the power of the relational database, and it could not be easier. All you have to do is create a new field in the Inventory table that will store the unique serial number of the category to which that item belongs. The unique serial number is in field zID of the Collections table; it is created and maintained by FileMaker. (There is also a zID field in the Inventory table and in almost every other table shown in this book.) Figure 5.7 shows how you can create this Category ID field.

NOTE

FileMaker can use text for the fields used in the relationship; if you want, you can use a category name as the field in the Inventory table. However, there are efficiencies in using numbers for the relationship. As you will see later in this chapter, the user need never see the number.

To complete the relationship, go to the Relationships tab of the Define Database dialog and draw a relationship between zID in Categories and Category ID in Inventory, as shown in Figure 5.8. (You can draw the relationship in either direction.)

FIGURE 5.7   **Create a**
`Category ID` **field in the**
`Inventory` **table.**

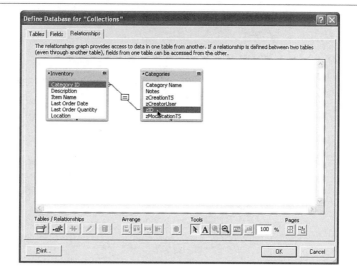

STEP 4 ▼
Creating the Category Report

You can build on the Inventory report from the previous project to create a report that is sorted by category. Start by going to that layout. You might notice that the new field you added, `Category ID`, has been automatically added to the layout, as shown in Figure 5.9.

FIGURE 5.9   New fields
are automatically added to
the current layout.

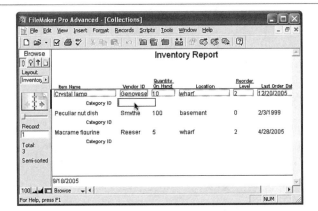

Go into Layout mode and remove that field
(and remember to tighten up the part that
might have been automatically enlarged).
That leaves the Inventory report as it was
before.

Now, still in Layout mode, duplicate that
layout (from the Layout menu). After that,
choose Layout Setup, as shown in Figure
5.10.

FIGURE 5.10   Rename the
layout.

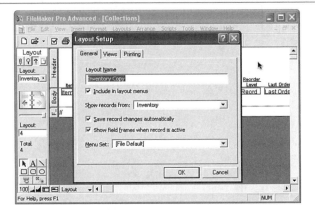

Rename the layout Categories (rather than
Inventory Copy). It is important to note that
you are building on the old Inventory report,
and so this layout is still based on the

Inventory table. That is correct. You will sort
it by category and show category names, but
the details of the report are from the
Inventory table.

NOTE

Layouts that are printed differ from layouts that are viewed on the computer screen in how related records are handled. For a printed report, the base table is the table containing the lowest level of data. If you have categories that contain inventory items, inventory items and their table are the base of the layout for a printed report.

For a report on the computer screen, related items can be shown in a *portal*—the scrolling list of related records that you can create. (You will create a portal in step 4 of Chapter 6.) As a result, the base table for a layout that contains a portal is the higher level of data. The comparable layout to this one that uses a portal would be based on the Categories table, and the related Inventory item records would be shown in a portal.

There is a simple explanation for this apparent inconsistency. When you print a portal, the image of the portal is printed. If the portal displays 10 rows and there are 500 other rows you could see by scrolling up or down in the portal, only the 10 visible rows are printed. In a report without a portal, all 510 data rows are printed.

Now you need to add the categories to the report. You could simply add the field containing the category name to each inventory record, but it is more useful to list all of the items for each category together. To do that, you need a sub-summary part.

The Part Setup command from the Layouts menu opens the dialog shown in Figure 5.11.

FIGURE 5.11   Open the Part Setup dialog.

Use the Create button to create a new part. As shown in Figure 5.12, it is a sub-summary part, and it is based on the Category Name field from the Categories table. (Use the drop-down menu at the top right of the dialog to select the table, and then select the appropriate field.) Note that the table must be sorted by this field.

FIGURE 5.12   Create the sub-summary part for the category name.

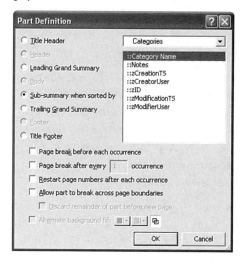

You can display the sub-summary above or below the detail data. The dialog shown in Figure 5.13 enables you to choose where to place the summary. (As shown in the figure, the default location is below the data, but you can choose to place it above the data by clicking Print Above.) The dialog is opened for you automatically when you create the sub-summary part.

FIGURE 5.13   Place the sub-summary above the data.

If you want the sub-summary to appear both above and below the data it summarizes, create two sub-summary parts based on the same field and place one above and the other below the data. (You might want the sub-summary to appear above the data with only some text, such as the name of the data summarized, and below the data with the text and summary values.)

The Part Setup dialog now reflects the new part, as shown in Figure 5.14. Note that you can rearrange parts in this dialog by dragging them up or down with the two-headed arrow. If you have multiple sub-summary parts, be careful that they are sorted in the order that they appear.

It is not enough to add the sub-summary part to the layout: You must add a field to it. Add the Category Name field from the Categories table to the sub-summary. You can set the style to bold and move it slightly to the left of the item name so the report looks better.

FIGURE 5.14   The sub-summary part is now added to the layout.

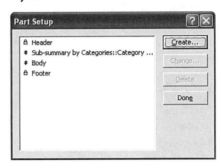

At this point, the new layout, based on the old Inventory layout, is complete. Two more steps will finish the job.

In creating the Inventory layout in the previous chapter, the New Layout/Report assistant generated a script to automatically sort the data and produce the report. Copy that script, and make two modifications:

▶ In the first line, change the Go To Layout script step to refer to the new layout with which you have been working.

▶ Double-click the Sort script step to modify the sort so the records are properly ordered for the new sub-summary part. If you add the Category Name field from the Categories table, you might find yourself with the sort order shown in Figure 5.15. Drag Categories::Category Name so that it is the first item in the sort order. That makes the sub-summary work properly; then, within each sub-summary break, the inventory items are sorted by name.

FIGURE 5.15 Make
certain the sort order is
correct.

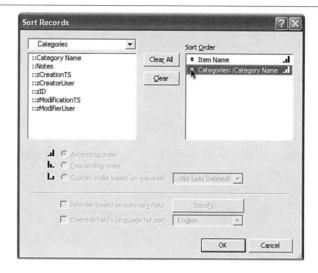

The final step is a clean-up step that makes your solution a little clearer when you or others use it. In Layout mode, choose Set Layout Order from the Layouts menu to open the dialog shown in Figure 5.16.

FIGURE 5.16 Remove the scripted layouts from the Layouts menu.

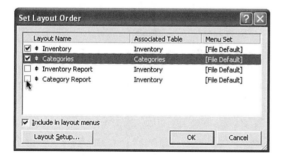

FileMaker has automatically created layouts for you with each table that is created. In addition, you have created two layouts (Inventory Report in the previous chapter and Category Report in this one). The two layouts you have created both have scripts to sort the data and generate the reports. If you select

either of those layouts from the Layouts menu in the Status Area without properly sorting the data, the results are undefined. To avoid confusion, use the Set Layout Order to remove those two layouts from the Layouts menu. That way, only the two data entry layouts appear.

STEP 5 ▼
Adding Categories to Data Entry

The Category layout is ready to go, but you need a way to enter category information for each item in the database. You do this by modifying the Inventory layout. Begin with a bit of clean-up. As shown in Figure 5.17, move the five administrative fields (those with names starting with z) into the footer of the layout. The auto-enter options you set for those fields do not allow data entry, so there is no reason for them to sit in the body of the report with the fields that can be entered.

Also, because they are of secondary importance, you can easily reduce their font size. Use the Align and Distribute submenus in the Arrange menu to organize them. (In FileMaker Pro 7, use the Set Alignment and Align commands in the Arrange menu to do this.)

The relationship between Inventory and Categories is based on a number—Category ID in Inventory and zID in Categories. This is an internal matter, and you should not show this to the user. Instead, users should work with category names.

To do this, create a *value list* using the Define Value Lists command in the File menu. This opens a list of the existing dialogs; from there you can edit a dialog or create a new one. Having chosen New or Edit, you now see the dialog shown in Figure 5.18.

FIGURE 5.17 **Move the non-entry fields to the bottom of the layout.**

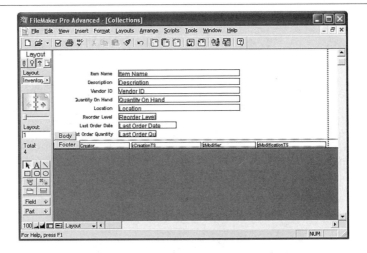

FIGURE 5.18 **Create a value list for categories.**

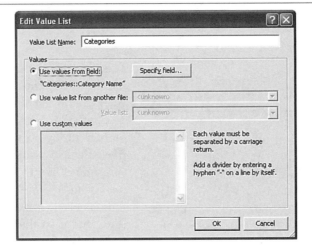

CHAPTER 5: Managing One-to-Many Relationships

When you choose the Use Values from Field option and click the OK button, you open the dialog shown in Figure 5.19. (Note that this is the FileMaker Pro 8 version; as noted in the following paragraph there is a functional difference between this version and FileMaker Pro 7.)

FIGURE 5.19 **Select the fields for the value list.**

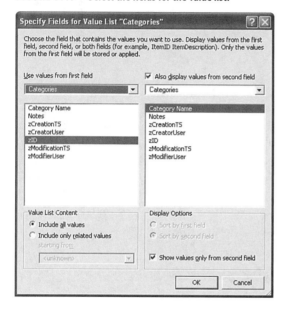

A value list contains values that will be used to set a field's value. In this case, the value is the values in the zID field of Categories. But FileMaker allows you to display another value from the record in which the primary field is located. Typically, this is used to display an intelligible version (such as Category Name) of an internally used value (such as zID). In FileMaker Pro 8, you can click the check box in the lower right so only the values in the second field are shown; in previous versions, you have to show both values and let the user ignore the numeric value.

Now that you have the value list in place, you can finish data entry. Go to the Inventory layout, and add the new field, Category ID, to the layout. (Depending on what layout was visible when you added the field to the Database Design dialog, it might already be there.) If you are using FileMaker Pro 8, you should add this field twice for testing purposes.

Use the Field Format command in the Format menu of Layout mode (FileMaker Pro 7) or the Field/Control Setup command (FileMaker Pro 8) to make this new field a drop-down menu attached to your value list, as shown in Figure 5.20.

If you have not entered any data for categories, switch to the Categories layout and enter one or more categories. All you have to do is create a new record and enter a category name. FileMaker automatically assigns the unique serial numbers.

Now, in the Inventory layout, you can use your drop-down menu to assign categories to inventory items. If you are using FileMaker Pro 8, the drop-down menu contains only the names of the categories. When you select one, the duplicate field that you created for testing will verify that, indeed, you have selected category 1, 5, or 99, even though the entire interface displays only text. If you are using FileMaker Pro 7, this second field is unnecessary because the number will appear next to the name in the drop-down menu.

Remember that the numeric data is used for the relationship.

FIGURE 5.20   Use the
value list as the basis for a
drop-down menu for data
entry into Category ID.

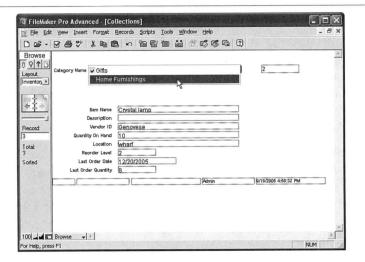

With that, you have finished adding categories to the database. The completed Inventory layout appears in Figure 5.21 as it is shown after the script is run to sort the data and use the new layout. The script ends by entering Preview mode. This presents the report as it will print: Summaries are adjusted and sliding fields have been slid. Until you click Continue in the status area, you are limited to printing the report, browsing from page to page (with the book icon), and scrolling up and down on each individual page.

FIGURE 5.21   Categories
are added to the Inventory
database.

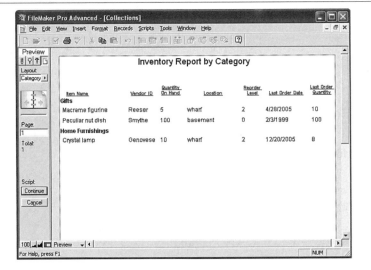

Final Thoughts

One step is sometimes necessary when you build a relationship that has not been included in this project because it does not apply to this data. Nevertheless, it is worth discussing. You can double-click the box in the middle of the relationship path between two tables to open a dialog that enables you to refine the relationship. So far, all of the relationships have been *equijoins*—equality between two values.

You can control how related data is affected by deletions if you want. For example, you can specify that deleting a category deletes all inventory items in that category. You also could specify that deleting an inventory item deletes the category to which it belongs. Neither choice is logical for this data; however, if you are modifying this project to use in other circumstances, those might be correct choices.

This project implements the basics of the relational model: Inventory items are related to categories in a many-to-one relationship (many inventory items can be related to a single category). But this is not always a reasonable restriction. While physical objects can only be in one place at a time, they (and digital objects) can logically be related to more than one category. In a boutique, a vase could be categorized as a gift, as a house furnishing, or even as a gardening item. The database design shown in this chapter does not work in that case. But the one in Chapter 6 will. It will show you how to implement many-to-many relationships.

Note that together with Chapter 4, these three chapters cover the basic structure of every relational database (not just FileMaker).

CHAPTER 6: Managing Many-to-Many Relationships

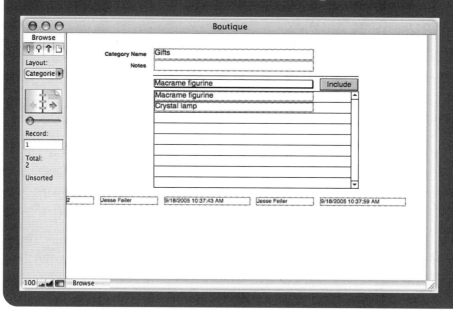

About the Project

This project produces a database in which a many-to-many relationship is implemented. Think of an eclectic boutique with three lamps of the same style. In one area, one lamp is in a display of lamps. In another corner, the lamp is in a display of furnishings for a child's room. Still elsewhere, the third lamp is in a collection of objects in various shades of blue. In preparing a database structure, in what category does that lamp belong: lamps, the child's room display, or blue objects? Clearly the lamp can be part of a number of collections, just as each collection can contain a number of objects. The one-to-many relationship in Chapter 5, "Managing One-to-Many Relationships," breaks down in this case. The project in this chapter handles that case.

Prerequisites

This project builds on the previous two projects.

@work resources

Please visit the publisher's website to access the following Chapter 6 files:

▶ Boutique.fp7

▶ Shell.fp7

Planning the Project

In this and the two previous projects, you have seen various combinations of *cardinality*—unrelated items, one-to-many relationships, and, now, many-to-many relationships. (The last permutation, many-to-many relationships, is also used in Chapter 9, "Implementing a Scheduling Solution.")

As you start to plan any database, you need to determine the nature of the relationship between every pair of tables in your database. This is part of the process of *normalization* that was described in Chapter 3, "Building FileMaker Solutions."

Project: Boutique Manager

We'll be creating a Boutique database solution in six easy steps:

STEPS ▼

1. Getting started
2. Setting up a join table
3. Creating the many-to-many relationship
4. Showing the relationships in a layout
5. Enabling data entry for the many-to-many relationship
6. Building the other end of the relationship

STEP 1 ▼
Getting Started

Begin by making a copy of the database from the previous project (you can download the completed database for this project from the website).

STEP 2 ▼
Setting Up a Join Table

The previous relationships were implemented using a field in a table that contained the unique identifier of a record in another table. You cannot do that in a many-to-many relationship because you need a varying number of fields to store the many relationships. (Do not even think of using a repeating field for this data!)

The key to many-to-many relationships is a small table called a *join table*. It contains the two identifying numbers for the two records it joins. You can see the join table you need in Figure 6.1. It has the same five administrative fields (beginning with *z*) that all tables in this project have. Create it either from scratch or by using FileMaker Pro Advanced and importing the Shell table as in the previous chapter. Add the Category ID and Item ID fields (they are both numbers).

FIGURE 6.1   **Create a join table.**

STEP 3 ▼
Creating the Many-to-Many Relationship

The Join table needs to be related to both the Inventory table and the Categories table. Because you are building on the project from the preceding chapter, there is already a relationship between the Inventory table and the Categories table (it is a many-to-one relationship). FileMaker allows you to create multiple relationships between pairs of tables, but you must identify them separately.

First, create the relationship between the zID field in Inventory and Item ID in the Join table, as shown in Figure 6.2.

Now, you need to create the relationship between the zID field in Categories and Category ID in the Join table. In almost every case, it does not matter how you draw relationships in the database graph—every relationship is bidirectional. In this particular case, however, the drawing direction matters. If you draw the relationship from the Categories table to the Join table, you get the dialog shown in Figure 6.3.

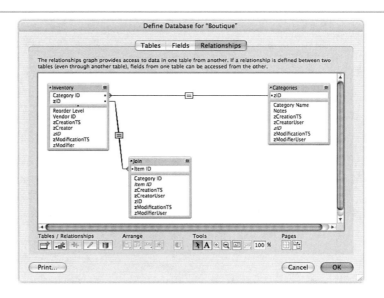

FIGURE 6.3 **FileMaker automatically creates alias tables to preserve the uniqueness of paths.**

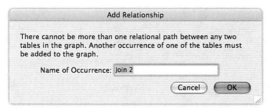

You can only have a single path between two of the tables in the database graph. But you can create an alias of a table. This alias points to the underlying table, but it provides a separate table in the database graph so you can build a relationship to it. If FileMaker detects a duplicate path between two tables, it offers to create an alias for you, as the Add Relationship dialog shows.

If you click OK, that alias table is created, and it is named Join 2 by default. Unfortunately, that does not solve your problem. You need a single table (alias or not) in the database graph that has relationship paths to both Inventory and Categories.

The solution is to draw the relationship from the Join table to Categories. Figure 6.4 shows that relationship being drawn just before the mouse button is released over the Categories table.

FileMaker still needs to create an alias table, but this time, it creates an alias to the Categories table, as shown in Figure 6.5.

FIGURE 6.4   Draw the relationship from the Join table to Categories.

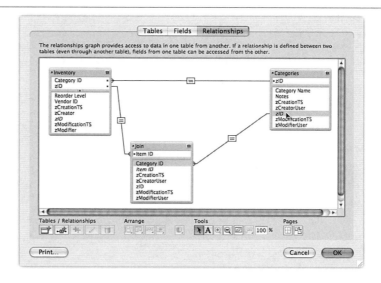

FIGURE 6.5   FileMaker creates an alias to the Categories table.

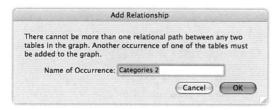

If you click OK, that alias is created as shown in Figure 6.6.

The Categories 2 alias points to the Categories table; there is no copy or duplication because it is the same table. But there is only one path from Inventory to Categories and only one path from Inventory to Categories 2 in the database graph. This allows you to use different relationships to the same data.

Most important, the Join table has relationships both to Inventory and to Categories (through the Categories 2 alias). You have created a many-to-many relationship.

You can rename any table in the database graph. Double-click on the Categories table to open the dialog shown in Figure 6.7.

FIGURE 6.6 **The**
Categories **table now has**
an alias in the database
graph.

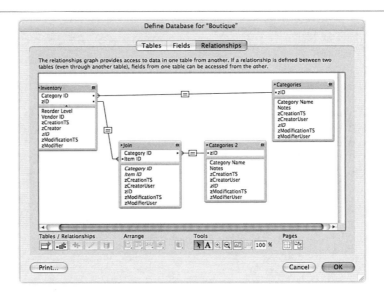

FIGURE 6.7 **Rename a table or change its underlying**
table.

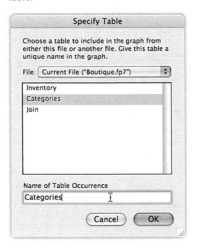

You can rename it Categories for 1TM (one-to-many); having done so, you can rename Categories 2 as Categories. (You also can change the underlying table.) The renamed database graph is shown in Figure 6.8.

Because you can use alias tables, the database schema now simultaneously has a one-to-many relationship between Inventory and Categories as well as the new many-to-many relationship. Because they have separately named tables and aliases, there is no confusion when you use them in layouts.

FIGURE 6.8 **Rename the tables in the database graph for clarity.**

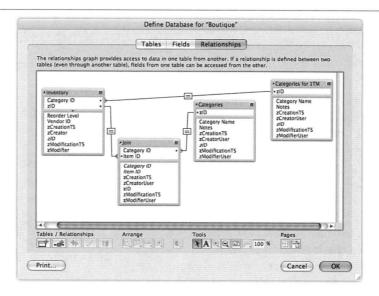

STEP 4 ▼
Showing the Relationships in a Layout

The database schema is now finished. You need to be able to display the relationships as well as to create them. This step modifies a layout for the first purpose; the next step enables you to create layouts.

 NOTE

When you are building solutions, you might choose to do the data entry before the data display or vice versa (as is the sequence here). Neither way is better, but some people feel that by working from the finished result—the report—they are able to make the data entry layout and scripts more focused on the needs of the report. Do whatever makes most sense to you as you go along.

Go into Layout mode and do some preparatory work. Because you already have an Inventory layout with the one-to-many relationship implemented, you might want to keep it. In the example file on the website, it has been renamed Inventory for 1 Category. In addition, a duplicate of that layout has been created and named Inventory.

You can rearrange the layout if you want (there is no need for the drop-down menu that enables you to choose a single category at the top). To display the various categories into which an individual item might fall, draw a portal. The dialog shown in Figure 6.9 enables you to set its parameters. Most important is to base it on the Join table.

FIGURE 6.9   Create a portal based on the Join table.

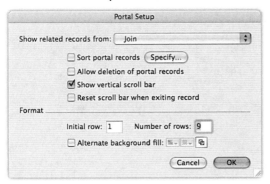

Next, you are prompted to add fields to the portal. You need not do this now because they can be added later, but it is easier to go ahead and add the Category Name field. Because the portal is located in a layout that is based on the Inventory table and that contains the item name, you only need to display the category name. A later step displays inventory item names in a portal for a given category.

FIGURE 6.10   Add the Category Name field to the portal.

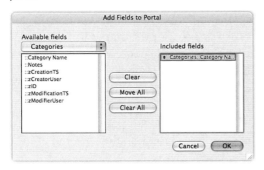

STEP 5 ▼
Enabling Data Entry for the Many-to-Many Relationship

Data entry consists of adding a record to the Join table with the unique ID numbers of a category and an inventory item. You can do it yourself with the default Join layout that FileMaker has created. Note the zID values for the inventory item and the category, create a new Join record, and enter them.

This is a good interface for testing and proving the concept, but it is not a good interface for users. Fortunately, it is simple to create a good interface, and creating Join table records is so common that you can use this process over and over:

1. Start from the Inventory layout from step 4.

2. Create a global field to temporarily store a category ID.

3. Use a value list to set that field.

4. Write a script to go to the Join table, create a new record, and set the two ID fields.

Add the field gTemp1 to the Inventory table. (Most people use a lower-case *g* to indicate global fields.) It is a number field, and its storage is global. Figure 6.11 shows how you set global storage using the Options dialog in the Define Database dialog.

FIGURE 6.11   **Create the** gTemp1 **numeric field; set its storage to global.**

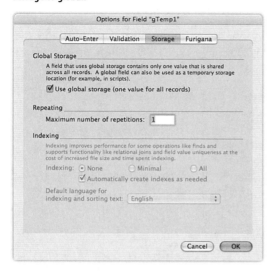

You created the value list in the previous project, so you can reuse it here. When you created gTemp1, FileMaker added it to the Inventory layout. Select that field and, using Field Control/Setup (FileMaker Pro 8) or Field Format (FileMaker Pro 7) from the Format

menu, assign the Categories value list to a drop-down menu in that field, just as you did in Chapter 5.

Finally, write the script. It is a very common script, and it is shown in Figure 6.12.

The script, like all good scripts, begins with comments indicating what it does and what parameters (if any) it expects. Note that one of these comments indicates that it has no interaction. This is important because if you want to reuse scripts, it is helpful to know which ones can safely be included in workflows that might run unattended.

In this case, two script parameters are expected. You can parse out individual values from a script parameter using the MiddleValues function as shown here. The GetAsNumber function converts the text of the script parameter into a number. If you are using text as a value in the script parameter, you need to write code to omit the ¶ symbol that separates all values, but if you use GetAsNumber, the ¶ symbol is automatically removed in the numeric conversion.

FIGURE 6.12   **Write the script.**

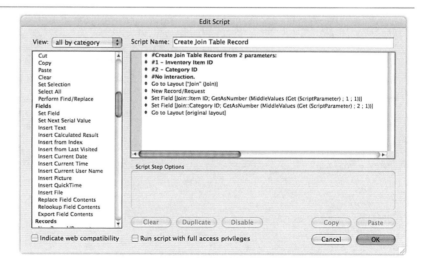

You go to the Join layout, create a new record, set the fields, and then return to the original layout.

Now it is simply a matter of putting things together. You have the global field that can

be set with the drop-down menu. Draw a button next to it and attach the script to it, as shown in Figure 6.13.

Choose the script you just wrote and click the Edit button, as shown in Figure 6.14.

FIGURE 6.13   **Attach a script to a button.**

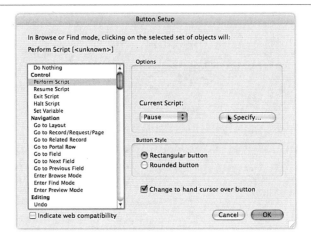

FIGURE 6.14   **Edit the script parameter.**

This opens the dialog shown in Figure 6.15. Construct the script parameter from the zID field and the gTemp1 field. If you are packing several values into a script parameter, remember to separate them with the ¶ symbol. It is usually a good idea to place them on separate lines, as shown in Figure 6.15.

Do any final rearrangement you want to the layout. In Figure 6.16, you can see that the button has been labeled and the section of the layout with the view of the portal and the drop-down menu for assigning a category has been separated slightly by a line. You can add categories to the inventory item as you want.

FIGURE 6.15   Create the
script parameter.

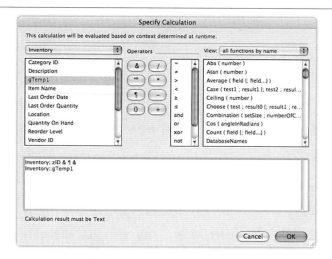

FIGURE 6.16   Test the
interface.

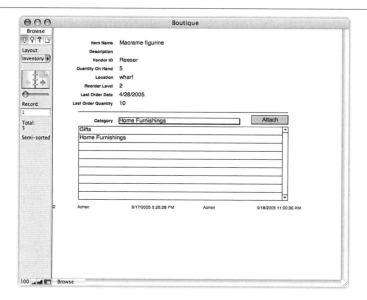

STEP 6 ▼
Building the Other End of the Relationship

There is a default layout for Categories that
FileMaker has created. It looks something
like Figure 6.17.

Rearrange the fields so it looks like the layout
for Inventory that was finished in Figure
6.16. Place the administrative fields in the
footer and make them smaller. You can look
at the modified layout in the database file
located on the website.

FIGURE 6.17   **Start from the default layout for Categories.**

Now create a copy of the layout. Use the Layout Setup command from the Layouts menu to change the base table to the Categories table that is accessed through the Join table, as shown in Figure 6.18.

FIGURE 6.18   **Set the layout base table to** Categories.

Then, in the same way that you created a portal for the Join table on the Inventory layout, create an identical portal on this one. The only difference is that instead of displaying the category name, you want the inventory name.

You now need a value list for inventory items; build it exactly as the category value list was built in Chapter 5.

The gTemp1 field has the new value list (of inventory items) attached to it. You need a button that invokes the same script as before. The only difference is that you are passing in the gTemp1 field (with the Inventory ID) followed by the zID field of the Categories table.

✦ NOTE

The gTemp1 **field that you created in the** Inventory **table can be reused here. Because it is a global field, whatever value it has is usable.**

The completed layout is shown in Figure 6.19.

You can add categories or inventory items using the respective layouts. From each one, you can create a relationship to a category or inventory item. Experiment and watch how each portal is automatically updated as a result of your edits.

FIGURE 6.19   **Test the completed layout.**

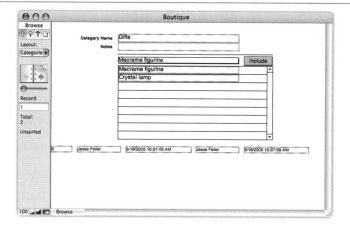

Final Thoughts

This chapter complete the sequence of three projects that implement the basic types of relationships. Now it is on to projects that track events over time, such as production management in Chapter 7, "Managing Production, Tasks, and Subtasks;" other features of FileMaker, such as the unified security model in Chapter 8, "Creating a Secure Shared Database;" and class enrollment in Chapter 9, in which additional processes are added to the categorization of data (such as payments).

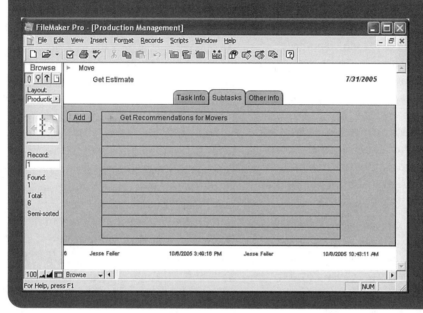

About the Project

This project adds time and manages tasks and subtasks. Each task and subtask has dates associated with it. On the database structure side, you will see how to manage hierarchical data; on the interface side, you will see how to handle dates and flag specific dates. You can use this project as the centerpiece of a more ambitious management solution that can track clients and inventory by combining the Production Management database with other databases.

Prerequisites

This project uses scripts, script parameters, tabbed layouts, dynamic formatting, variables, and drop-down calendars, some of which are new in FileMaker Pro 7 and 8. You might want to review these features before starting this project.

@work resources

Please visit the publisher's website to access the following Chapter 7 files:

- ▶ **Production Management.fp7**
- ▶ **Shell.fp7**
- ▶ **Triangle.jpg**

Planning the Project

When people approach a project such as this one, they usually become bogged down in the idea of tasks and subtasks (and subtasks of subtasks). One way of allowing for such a hierarchical structure is to create separate tables for tasks and subtasks. But if you choose this route, you need additional tables for subtasks of subtasks. Another way of dealing with the hierarchical structure is to force the data into a structure that is limited to a certain number of levels (such as two). Forcing the data into a structure is usually not a good idea: The structure should accommodate the data, not vice versa.

The solution to a database design problem such as this is two-fold. First of all, recognize that there is nothing intrinsically different between a task and a subtask. Both have a name, a start date, a promised date, and a completed date. (In the real world, there might be some minor differences—perhaps in how time is billed—but they can be handled by adding fields to the database that are not always filled with data.) The biggest issue is that a subtask always has a parent task, and that turns out to be a minor issue.

After you have determined that there is no basic difference between tasks and subtasks, the database structure evolves very easily if you use self-joins. A *self-join* is a relationship that joins a table to itself. In order to create a self-join, you need to create an alias to the table so you see two tables in the FileMaker relationship graph. Both of those tables are based on the same database table. But because you now have two apparent tables in the relationship graph, you can draw a relationship between them.

As you will see in this project, the heart of the database design is two aliased tables added to the original table in the relationship graph. One relationship goes from the Production Management table to an alias based on a relationship to the parent task; this aliased table is called Parent Task. From the original task to the parent, the relationship is a many-to-one relationship: Each task can have only one parent task, but a single parent might have many tasks under it. Likewise, a relationship from the Tasks table goes to an alias called Sub Tasks. When you look at the database diagram, you see the parent task, the main task, and that task's subtasks. These are all based on the same table, and when you switch from one table to another in a layout, you switch your perspective. Any task can be a parent, a main task, or a subtask, depending on how you view it.

Both of these relationships are based on a Parent Task field and the zID field. Any task that has a parent has a value in the Parent Task field, and that value matches the zID value in the parent task. Do not worry about a subtask field. In a main task, the zID value relates to the Parent Task field in its subtasks.

This is the major database planning issue for this project. As you work through the project, you will see how it is implemented.

Two other issues are dealt with in the project. The first is the use of a container field called Other Information. This field allows you to add a file, a picture, a movie, or other information to any task's record. It provides additional information (as well as a way to illustrate yet another FileMaker feature).

Also, there is a global field called gDateTestField. The dates displayed in the layouts are automatically modified to change color when they are past due. One way of doing this is to create calculations that check if the date values are less than the current day's date (in other words, past due). A more flexible way is to use a global field with the date to be tested. At startup time, a script can set that field to the current day's date, but you can change the global value at any time so the coloring of the data reflects last week, next month, or any other specified date.

> ### ✒ NOTE
> A substantive issue can be involved with the assumption that there can only be a single parent task for a given task. Certain organizations and certain times allow for joint management of project phases. In most of these cases, however, a new entity (a committee or task force) is formed, and this entity, composed of managers from more than one area, is the single manager. Likewise, in determining a task's parent task, a new coordinator task might need to be considered.

Project: Production Management

We'll be creating a Production Management solution in 11 easy steps:

STEPS ▼

1. Getting started
2. Adding the fields
3. Cleaning up the layout
4. Creating the self-join relationships
5. Creating the tabbed layout
6. Adding fields to the Task Info tab
7. Adding the portal to the Subtasks tab
8. Implementing navigation
9. Creating the script and adding the button to add new subtasks
10. Adding the drop-down calendar
11. Coloring the date

STEP 1 ▼
Getting Started

Begin by creating the database. If you have FileMaker Pro 8, you can create that database and import the Shell table into it. If not, copy the Shell database. In either case, you wind up with a database with one table in it (the Shell table). That table has the five administrative fields filled in automatically, as shown in Figure 7.1 Rename the Shell table as Production Management.

STEP 2 ▼
Adding the Fields

In the Production Management table, you now need to add the fields that will be used in this project, as shown in Figure 7.1.

There are two text fields for each task:

▶ **Task Name**—You should use the Options button to require that the Task Name field not be empty. You can set an auto-enter option so each new task is entitled New Task. This means that Task Name will not be empty unless the user accidentally erases it. Obviously, if you use this set of choices, you must allow for duplicate task names.

▶ **Notes**—Add any information you need to keep track of here.

 TIP

Many designers automatically add a Notes field to each record in a database. FileMaker is very good about not wasting space: If no data is in a Notes field, it takes up very little space in the database. And if there is something unusual about a task (or any other entity that is represented in a FileMaker database), the Notes field is useful.

There are three date fields; their names are self-explanatory:

▶ Date Started

▶ Date Promised

▶ Date Finished

A container field, Other Information, can be used to store a file, a file reference, a graphic, a movie, or any other data of that type.

FIGURE 7.1 Add the fields.

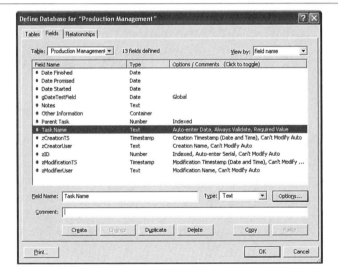

To implement the self-join relationships described previously, you need a field for the zID value of the parent of a task—Parent Task (this is a number).

Finally, you need the global field, gDateTestField, in which to store that date—often today's date—that is used for calculating whether a task is late.

STEP 3 ▼
Cleaning Up the Layout

Depending on the sequence in which you created the fields, the default layout might look somewhat messy. Starting in step 5, you will be building a new layout. However, in the interim you might want to clean up the layout you have. If you want, you can omit this step.

There are two ways to tidy the layout. One way is to rearrange the fields and their labels. The other (often easier) way is to create a new layout, and allow the New Layout/Report assistant to start from scratch. You should move all of the fields to the new layout; rearrange them in the scrolling list at the right, as shown in Figure 7.2, to minimize the amount of time you will need to fiddle with them later.

FIGURE 7.2   Order the fields in the layout.

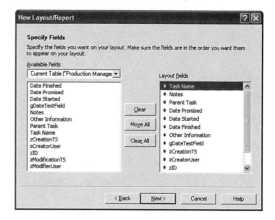

The five administrative fields (starting with z) provide you with information that is automatically set by FileMaker and that can provide you with help in diagnosing problems. You can delete the field names and place the fields themselves in the footer of the layout. You also can set their font size to the smallest size that is comfortable for you to read. Align their tops (or bottoms), and distribute them across the footer. Not having labels on those fields will not cause a problem if you always use them in the same sequence in your layouts.

When you have cleaned up the layout a bit, it might look like the layout shown in Figure 7.3.

If you created a new layout in this step (rather than cleaning up the existing layout), you might want to delete the old layout.

FIGURE 7.3   Clean up the
layout.

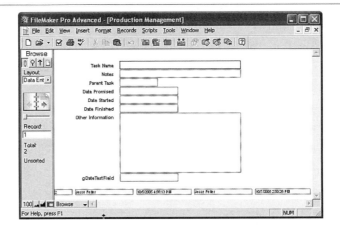

STEP 4 ▼
Creating the Self-join Relationships

Now you need to create two self-join relationships. They must be in place before you start
to build the final layout in the next step. In
the Relationships tab of the Define Database
dialog, create a new table using the New
Table button in the lower left. The dialog
shown in Figure 7.4 opens. You need to
specify the table on which this new table will
be based: select Production Management.
Each table in the database graph must have
a unique name; because Production
Management is already the name of a table,
FileMaker suggests a new name, as the figure
shows. You can improve on this. Change the
name of this new table to Parent Task.

FIGURE 7.4   **Create a new table based on** Production
Management.

Repeat the process to create a new table
based on Production Management and called
Sub Tasks. Create the relationships by
drawing a relationship from Parent Task in
Sub Tasks to zID in Production Management
and a second relationship from Parent ID in
Production Management to zID in Parent
Tasks. Figure 7.5 shows the completed database graph.

FIGURE 7.5 **Draw the relationships.**

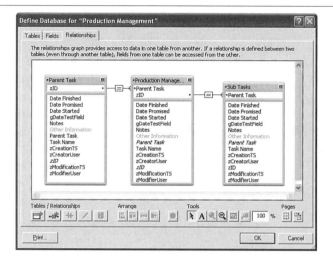

STEP 5 ▼
Creating the Tabbed Layout

In this step, you begin to create a layout with a tab control. This provides you with three tabs (Task Info, Subtasks, and Other Info) that display the data. As you will see, the Subtasks tab consists of a portal to the Sub Tasks table.

Create a new blank layout and put the five administrative fields into the footer. Alternatively, copy the layout you have used so far and which, in step 3, you used to arrange those administrative fields in the footer. In this scenario, delete all of the fields except for those in the footer.

Use the Layout Setup command to make certain that this new layout is based on the Production Management table.

Making Tabs in FileMaker 7

Tab controls are implemented in FileMaker 8. If you are using FileMaker 7, you need to implement tabs by creating them in separate layouts. The simplest way to do this is to design the first layout with all tabs visible and the rest of the layout in place. (Create tabs by drawing rounded-rectangle buttons. Draw a heavy horizontal line across the bottom, and they appear as flat-bottomed tabs.)

Write a script and then attach it to each one of the tabs. Add a script parameter so 1 is passed into the script on tab 1, 2 for tab 2, and so forth.

Then, duplicate the layout once for every tab. At this point, you should rename each of the copies, indicating which tab is active. Modify the script so that when the script parameter is 1, you go to the layout for tab 1, 2 sends you to the layout for tab 2, and so on.

Finally, adjust each of the duplicated layouts so the active tab is highlighted. You also should remove the script from that tab.

Or upgrade to FileMaker Pro 8.

Add two fields to the header: Task Name and Parent Task::Task Name. These can be added with the Insert Merge Field command. Figure 7.6 shows the layout at this stage with

- ▶ The administrative fields in the footer
- ▶ The Task Name and Parent Task::Task Name fields inserted as merge fields in the header

Using either the Tab Control command from the Insert menu or the Tab Control tool in the status area, create a tab control. If you use the tool in the status area, you draw the tab control; after you do so, the Tab Control Setup dialog shown in Figure 7.7 opens. If you use the command, the Tab Control Setup dialog opens immediately, and the new tab control is drawn for you. In either case, you can move, resize, and reshape the tab control.

FIGURE 7.6 **Prepare the basics of the Tabbed layout.**

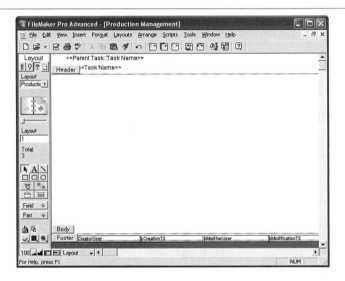

Set up the three tabs as shown in the dialog. Type each name in the Tab Name text box, and then click the Create button to create it in the list. Use the double-headed arrows to move tab items up or down if you need to. When you have finished, click OK.

FIGURE 7.7 **Open the Tab Control Setup dialog.**

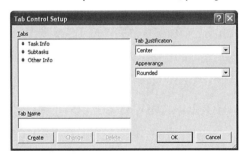

STEP 6 ▼
Adding Fields to the Task Info Tab

As shown in Figure 7.8, add fields to the Task Info tab. The fields you add here should be

- ▶ Task Name
- ▶ Notes
- ▶ Date Started
- ▶ Date Promised
- ▶ Date Finished

FIGURE 7.8 **Add fields to the Task Info tab.**

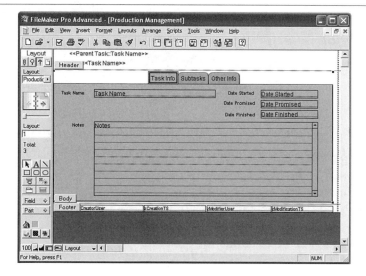

STEP 7 ▼
Adding the Portal to the Subtasks Tab

Select the Subtasks tab and draw a portal in it as shown in Figure 7.9. The portal should be based on the Sub Tasks table. It should contain a single field—Sub Tasks::Task Name. Leave a little space at the left of the name as shown in the figure. A navigation icon will go there. Specify the number of rows you want in the portal. This is based on the data itself (there is no need to have 10 rows if you rarely have more than 3 rows of data); it is also based on the default screen size for which you are designing. People usually don't mind scrolling within a portal, but if they have to scroll the whole layout (containing the portal) up and down to see it all in one window's view, they might be irritated.

FIGURE 7.9 Draw the
Subtasks portal.

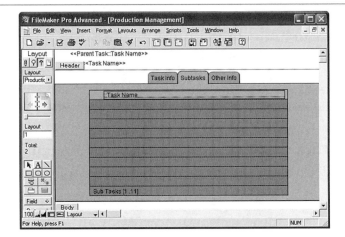

STEP 8 ▼
Implementing Navigation

It is important that you are able to quickly move from one task to another, particularly from subtask to parent task and vice versa. Navigation triangles are a commonly

accepted tool for moving to another record. A blue navigation triangle is provided in `triangle.jpg`, available on the publisher's website in the Chapter 7 section.

Insert it three times in the layout as shown in Figure 7.10.

FIGURE 7.10 Insert three
navigation triangles in the
layout.

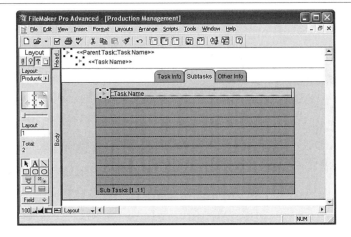

Click in the background to deselect the three triangles in Figure 7.10. Now, select the navigation triangle for the parent task, and use the Button Setup command in the Format menu to open the Button Setup dialog. Choose Go to Related Record from the scrolling list at the left, and then choose Specify in the Options box at the right. This opens the Go to Related Record Options dialog shown in Figure 7.11. Choose the following options:

► Get the related record from:
  Parent Task

► Show record using layout: Production Management

► Show only related records

FIGURE 7.11 **Set the options for Go to Related Record.**

When you click OK, you are taken back in the Button Setup dialog; it should now look like Figure 7.12.

FIGURE 7.12 **Set Button Setup options.**

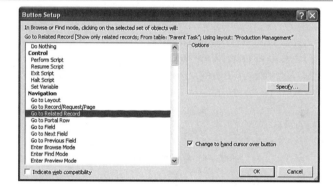

Select the navigation triangle for the task in the portal. Repeat the process, but make these choices:

► Get related record from: Sub Tasks

► Show record using layout: Production Management

► Show only related records

STEP 9 ▼
Creating the Script and Adding the Button to Add New Subtasks

Navigation has been enabled, but because you do not have an easy way to add subtasks, you cannot prove it. A simple script enables you to add subtasks as needed.

> **NOTE**
>
> It has long been the practice to add records to portals simply by entering data into a blank record at the bottom of the portal. This works without problems for portals that display single equijoin relationships. All relationships before FileMaker Pro 7 were of this nature; now only some of them are. Despite the fact that this relationship is, indeed, a single equijoin relationship, the script method of adding records to the portal is used. It works in all cases, whereas the blank-record-at-the-bottom method only works in some cases. From a user's point of view, it is better to become familiar with an interface (button and script) that always works rather than trying to remember which interface is used where.

Using ScriptMaker from the Scripts menu, create the script shown in Figure 7.13.

The script has six steps. The third and fourth do the work. The first step goes to the layout with which it works. At the end of the script, you return to the original layout. Those two steps are common. However, in a script such as this one where you add records to the table shown in the layout, sometimes you want to return not just to the original layout but to the actual record you were viewing in that layout. The record that is added is shown in a portal in the main layout, but you want to return to the original record with its original portal into which the new record has been placed. If you do not do this, you go to the new record that has been created (which is the record that is shown in the portal of the original record). You can try deleting steps 2 and 6 of the script to see what happens. This particular behavior is caused by the fact that this is a self-join, and the records in the portal are, indeed, records from the base table. But the general case (wanting to return not only to the original layout but also to the original record) is common enough; the solution shown here is used in any of the general cases.

FIGURE 7.13 **Create a script to add a subtask.**

```
Add Subtask from Script Parameter
Go to Layout [ "Production Management" (Production Management) ]
Set Variable [ $curRecordNumber; Value:Get ( RecordNumber ) ]
New Record/Request
Set Field [ Production Management::Parent Task; GetAsNumber ( MiddleValues ( Get ( ScriptParameter); 1; 1) ) ]
Go to Layout [ original layout ]
Go to Record/Request/Page [ $curRecordNumber ]
    [ No dialog ]
```

Variables are new in FileMaker Pro 8, and this script provides a good example of a situation in which you can use a local variable. You need to keep track of the record you started from at the beginning of the script so you can return to it. A local variable (one whose name starts with a single $) does the trick. It is available at all times in the script after you have defined it, but it disappears when the script terminates. In the cases in which you need to store data that lasts beyond the execution of a script, a global variable (one in which the name begins with $$) can be used; it is available to any script after it has been set. Beware of using global variables excessively. True global variables can replace global fields that you might have stored in a table for preferences; but in some cases, global variables can actually be redefined as local variables and automatically disposed of when their work is done. That makes for simpler code because the fewer global objects you deal with, the better off you are (for one thing, it is fewer things that you have to remember).

Figure 7.14 shows the setting of the global variable in this script.

FIGURE 7.14   Create a global variable.

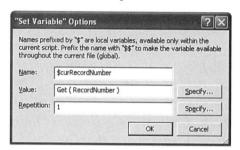

The script performs the following steps:

1. It goes to the Production Management layout. (It is being run from the layout now, but it might not always be.)

2. It stores the current record number in a local variable ($curRecordNumber).

3. It creates a new record.

4. It assumes that it contains a parameter with the ID number of what will be the parent record; it sets the `Parent ID` field of the newly created record to that value. Although there is only one value passed into the script parameter, this step uses the `MiddleValues` function to parse that single value out. This makes the script reusable in case more values are added.

5. It returns to the original layout. This is unnecessary in this particular case, but it makes the script reusable.

6. It returns to the original record, using the $curRecordNumber local variable.

Now draw a button next to the portal as shown in Figure 7.15. Label the button as Add, and attach the script to it. Remember to set the parameter for the script at the bottom of the Specify Script Options dialog as shown in Figure 7.15.

FIGURE 7.15   Attach the script to the button.

STEP 10 ▼
Adding the Drop-down Calendar

In FileMaker Pro 8, drop-down calendars are implemented for date fields. You can easily add this interface element to the date fields.

In Layout mode go to the Task Info tab of the Production Management layout. Select the three date fields and, from the Format menu, choose Field/Control and then Setup to open the dialog shown in Figure 7.16. Select Drop-down Calendar from the Display As drop-down menu. You might want to add borders to fields to outline them. Otherwise, the outlines are shown only when the user clicks in a field for data entry. The choice is yours.

In Figure 7.17, you can see the revised interface in action.

FIGURE 7.16 Add drop-down calendars to the date fields.

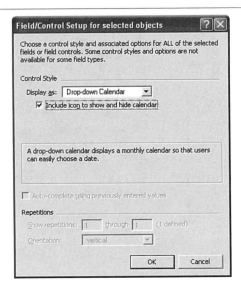

FIGURE 7.17 Drop-down calendars make date entry easier and prevent errors caused by typing invalid dates.

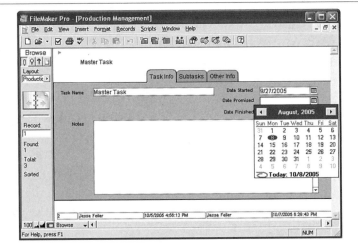

CHAPTER 7: Managing Production, Tasks, and Subtasks

STEP 11 ▼
Coloring the Date

You can use the FileMaker text-formatting functions to change attributes of text, including its color. To make this automatic, you can create calculation fields that display the contents of other fields and that apply formatting to them based on various calculations.

For this to work, you need to have separate fields for entering data and for displaying it because the display shows the calculated fields with appropriate formatting.

In the layout that you have, this is not hard to do. The date fields are entered in the Task Info tab, and they remain as they are. You can color any or all of the three dates; the one that is most likely to be colored is the Date Promised field. You can set it to red if the date is past. (For a variation, you could set it to yellow if the date is within a week of being past.)

Here is where the gDateTestField comes into play: It contains the as-of or comparison date, normally today's date. You need to set it to the default value and provide an interface to allow the date to be changed.

The easiest method to set the field to a default value is to create a script that is run automatically when the file is opened. The script is shown in Figure 7.18.

Use the File Options command in the File menu to set the script to run automatically when the file is opened, as shown in Figure 7.19.

FIGURE 7.18 **Create a script to set default values in fields if they need to change to reflect the current date.**

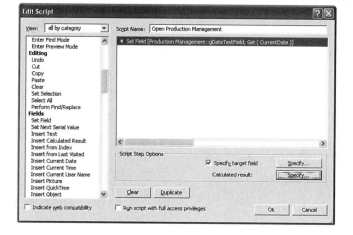

FIGURE 7.19   Run the script automatically when the file is opened.

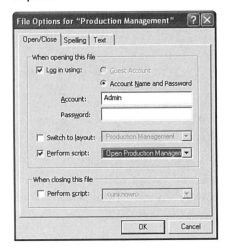

NOTE

You might wonder about the choice of a custom dialog to set the as-of date. Data that is used routinely belongs in layouts, not hidden in dialogs and scripts that only reveal themselves at certain times. But this date, the as-of date for date comparisons, is set by default to today's date at startup time, and most likely that date will be used. Because this field is only rarely changed, it is appropriate to hide it in a custom dialog and not to clutter the standard layouts with it.

If the project were to evolve so a number of preferences and comparison values were needed, you might consider a new layout that is used only to set these items. However, with only a single value in this category now, the custom dialog is fine.

Finally, to allow the user to modify the as-of date, you can provide a custom dialog as shown in Figure 7.20. A custom dialog can be created in a script as described in Chapter 2, "Automating FileMaker." To use this dialog you need a one-step script that displays the dialog and sets the field. (The field does not need to be in the current layout, but the current layout must be based on the table that contains the field—Production Management.)

The last step is to create a calculation field that displays the date in color if the date is past. Figure 7.21 shows the formula for that calculation field.

FIGURE 7.21   Create a calculation field to color the date.

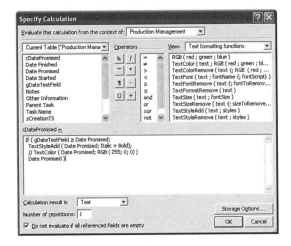

FIGURE 7.20   Use a custom dialog to set the as-of date.

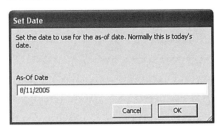

In the formula, the code to color the text has been commented out; in its place, code is provided to change the text style to bold and italic. Red is more noticeable on the screen, but in a book without color, the bold and italic display is more noticeable. You have both lines of code to use as you see fit.

The finished result is shown in Figure 7.22.

FIGURE 7.22 The project is finished.

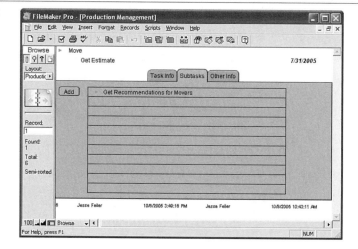

Final Thoughts

This project has covered a number of interface features you can use in a variety of circumstances. In addition, you have seen how to use self-join relationships and alias tables to switch rapidly from one section of data to another.

CHAPTER 8: Creating a Secure Shared Database

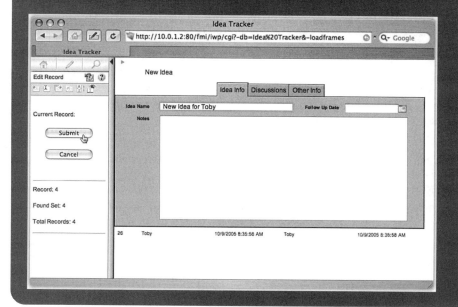

About the Project

This project expands on Chapter 7, "Managing Production, Tasks, and Subtasks." In the case of project or production management, the database is a management tool. In Idea Tracker, the database is the project itself. It might be an online discussion group, an internal brainstorming tool, or other types of idea manager. Its contents are the product of the process and formalize interaction and collaboration. Security for this project needs to be much higher than that of the previous one, and the database needs to be networked.

This project gives you an online or local project that enables you to manage ideas in a hierarchical or chronological manner while respecting the security needs of the online and networked worlds.

Prerequisites

This project's database design and basic layouts are those from Production Management in the previous chapter.

@work resources

Please visit the publisher's website to access the following Chapter 8 files:

▶ **Idea Tracker.fp7**

Planning the Project

The database design planning for this project is very similar to that of the previous project. Ideas can be tracked and grouped into topics; within a given idea, there can be a number of discussions. Thus, you have the same three-level hierarchy as before; the only difference is the naming. From top to bottom, the names are

- Topics
- Ideas
- Discussions

Each can be contained within the higher entity.

As noted previously, this project needs a higher level of security than previous projects because it is designed to be used interactively over a network—either a FileMaker network or the Internet itself. Planning for security has to start as early as possible in a project. In fact, planning for security might need to

proceed at the same time that the database plan takes shape.

In this project, a privilege set is created that most participants will use. It allows for the following:

- Unlimited viewing of data
- Modification of ideas you have entered
- Deletion of ideas you have entered and to which no one has added discussions

The last point is one of three solutions for handling deletion of related records in a related database. These are your choices:

- You can refuse to delete records to which other records are related.
- You can allow deletion of records without restriction. That might or might not leave orphan records that might contain incomplete or illogical data.
- You can not allow any deletions, which makes the whole issue moot.

None of these solutions is proper in all cases. Here, the first one (which is the most complex to implement) is used in part to illustrate how to handle this case. Note that the issues involved in implementing this logic are also useful in other security cases using FileMaker's unified security model.

Project: Idea Tracker

We'll be creating an Idea Tracker solution in seven easy steps:

STEPS ▼

1. Getting started
2. Modifying the database: changing fields
3. Modifying the database: renaming tables
4. Modifying the database: layouts and scripts
5. Setting account privileges
6. Setting up networking
7. Testing Instant Web Publishing

STEP 1 ▼
Getting Started

To start, you can use the completed database from the previous project. As noted, the database structure is the same; there is merely some renaming to be done. This step provides you with a guide to what you have to change and what you do not have to change to repurpose the database. FileMaker keeps track of its own data using internal identification numbers. Thus, a layout is referred to by FileMaker by a unique identifier. If you change the name of the layout using the Layout Setup command in the Layouts menu, that is all you need to do. FileMaker displays the new name in Go To Layout script steps, in the Layouts menu, and wherever else it appears.

 NOTE

This happens to provide a good example of why it is good database practice to always use unique, internal identifiers for objects in a database—name changes do not break relationships that are based on such meaningless identifiers as the `zID` and `Parent ID` fields used in these projects.

Begin by changing the name of the database file (before opening it) to `Idea Tracker`. Then, open the database and choose Define Database from the File menu. In the Tables tab, select Production Management, and, at the bottom of the dialog, rename it Ideas and click Change.

STEP 2 ▼
Modifying the Database: Changing Fields

The `Date Started` and `Date Finished` fields are not needed. Delete them.

Change the name of the `Task Name` field to `Idea Name`.

Change the name of `Data Promised` to `Follow Up Date`. In the case of an idea, that name makes more sense. (Keeping names accurately descriptive is always a challenge in modifying software, but it is very important so that you and your successors do not forget what the data actually is.) You will notice that when you change the name of `Date Promised` to `Follow Up Date`, the formula for `cDatePromised` is updated to use the new name. However, `cDatePromised` no longer accurately reflects its contents, so change its name to `cFollowUpdate`.

Finally, remember to change the auto-enter value for the Idea Name field to New Idea.

Figure 8.1 shows the Fields tab of the Define Database dialog with these changes made.

FIGURE 8.1 Rename fields in the Define Database dialog.

STEP 3 ▼
Modifying the Database: Renaming Tables

While the Define Database dialog is open, go to the Relationships tab. The new field names are shown. However, the table names remain the old ones. Double-click the top of each table to open the Specify Table dialog as shown in Figure 8.2.

Change the names as follows:

▸ Parent Tasks becomes Topics.

▸ Sub Tasks becomes Discussions.

▸ Production Management was renamed Ideas in the first step, so you do not need to do anything for it.

FIGURE 8.2   Change the table names.

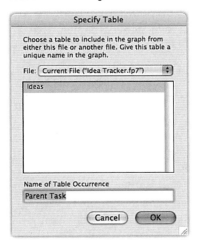

The database graph should appear as shown in Figure 8.3.

FIGURE 8.3   Change the
database graph.

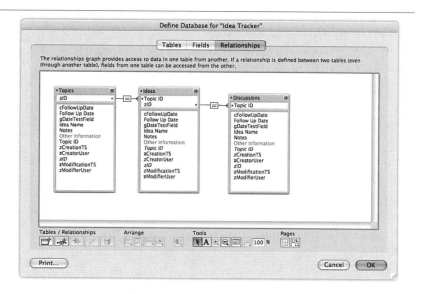

STEP 4 ▼
Modifying the Database:
Layouts and Scripts

When you go into Layout mode, you will see
that all of the field names have been
changed in the layouts because FileMaker is
working with its own internal identifiers. The
only changes you need to make at this time
are those that are typed into layouts. If you
have used FileMaker to create field names (as
opposed to typing them in yourself or
placing them on an inserted graphic), those
field names are changed for you.

What is not changed for you are instances of
text such as the tab names. Open the Tab
Control dialog by double-clicking the background of the tab control area or by choosing
Tab Control Setup from the Format menu. In
either case, change the names of the first two
tabs as shown in Figure 8.4.

FIGURE 8.4   Change the tab names.

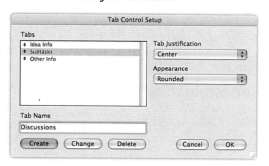

Finally, use ScriptMaker in the Scripts menu
to change the name of the Add Subtask from
Script Parameter script to Add Discussion
from Script Parameter. You do not need to do
this for the database to function correctly, but
it means that the script name now accurately
reflects the new nomenclature.

The steps in the project so far are the steps
that you should always check when reusing a
database for another purpose.

STEP 5 ▼
Setting Account Privileges

From the File menu, choose Define Accounts & Privileges. In the Privilege Sets tab, choose New to open the Edit Privilege Set dialog shown in Figure 8.5.

This is the privilege set that is used by participants in Idea Tracker. It has more privileges than the default Read-Only privilege set, and it has fewer than the Full Access privilege set. Specifically, it implements the deletion logic described previously in this chapter.

Name the privilege set (in the upper left) and provide a description of it. Set the options at the right of the dialog as you want. Later on in this project, you will provide networking for this solution, so now is a good time to turn on Instant Web Publishing and FileMaker Network extended privileges in the Extended Privileges box.

The most important setting is the Records setting in Data Access and Design. When you choose Custom Privileges, the Custom Record Privileges dialog shown in Figure 8.6 automatically opens.

FIGURE 8.5   Choose overall privilege settings.

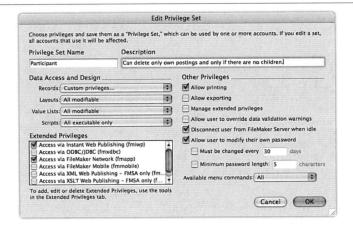

FIGURE 8.6   Set custom record privileges.

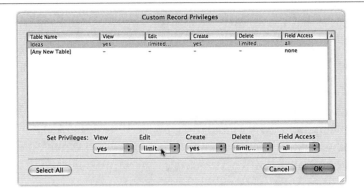

In each case, you can choose full, limited, or no access. Select the Ideas table. For View and Create, you want full access: The choice is Yes in the drop-down menus at the bottom of the dialog. For Field Access, the full-access choice is All.

For Edit, choose Limited as shown in Figure 8.6. This automatically opens the Specify Calculation dialog shown in Figure 8.7.

Any rules that you can specify in a calculation to be evaluated at run time can be used

to control access. In this case, there is a single rule: The creator of the record (zCreatorUser) must be the same as the current user. In other words, users with the Participant privilege set can only edit their own records.

Now you need to implement the more complex rule for Delete access. Choose limit from the drop-down menu under Delete to open the Specify Calculation dialog shown in Figure 8.8.

FIGURE 8.7 Specify the calculation to control Edit access.

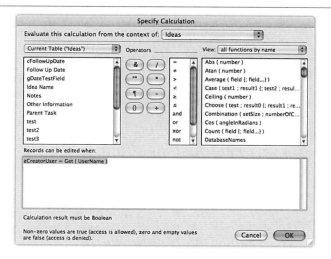

FIGURE 8.8 Specify the calculation to control Delete access.

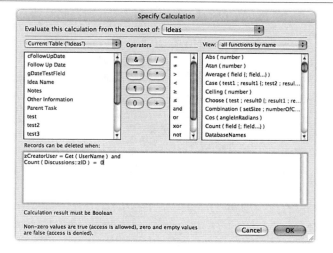

This calculation implements two rules. The first is that you can only delete records you created. But a second rule also applies. It uses the Count function to count the number of related records. It does this by counting the values for a field that is known to exist in every record—zID. (This is one side-benefit of auto-entering a value: You can rely on its presence in every record and use it to test for a relationship's existence.)

Both of these rules must be true to allow for the deletion of a record.

 NOTE

Note that the rules are combined with and. In English, the ampersand (&) means the same thing as *and*, but in computer languages, and is used for logical connections (both must be true) whereas & is used to combine text strings (concatenation). Because FileMaker automatically does data conversions for you, using & would cause the rule to behave erratically as it evaluates two text strings, not two logical values.

Click OK to close the Specify Calculation dialog. Now move to the Accounts tab and create a new account as shown in Figure 8.9. Assign it to the Participant privilege you have just created.

FIGURE 8.9 Create a new account.

You can assign any number of accounts to a privilege set.

If you log in using the new account you have created, you will be using the Participant privilege set. If you try to delete a record created by someone else or a record that has related discussion records, you will get the error message shown in Figure 8.10.

FIGURE 8.10 The Participant privilege set prevents you from deleting a record improperly.

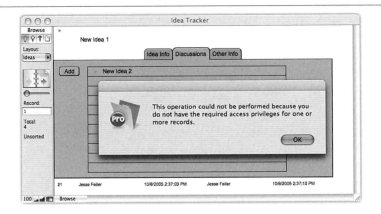

This dialog raises an issue because it is not specific as to the reason that you cannot delete the record. In fact, it merely refers to "this operation," so you cannot be entirely certain that it is the deletion that you cannot do.

You can implement your own error checking; this allows you to provide a customized error message. However, there are some disadvantages to this:

▶ You must remember to do it in your scripts. Blocking access using a privilege set is automatically done every time.

▶ You must implement commands, such as delete, in scripts that can do the error checking and remember to disable the corresponding menu commands.

Because implementing controls and edits in privilege sets, as well as in non-overrideable validation routines, means total automatic implementation of the rules, many people think that the benefit outweighs the ambiguity of the generated error messages.

As you close out of the Define Accounts & Privileges dialog, you might be warned of blank passwords (by default the password for the default admin account is blank), and you are prompted to enter a full-access account and password to make certain you do not lock yourself out of the file.

The last step in implementing security is to turn off the automatic log in to the admin account; this is set in File Options. After it is turned off, you can log in as admin or as one of the accounts you have created using your own or a default privilege set.

STEP 6 ▼
Setting Up Networking

To allow users to share the database over a network, use the Sharing submenu from the FileMaker Pro menu (on Mac OS X) or the Edit menu (on Windows).

The FileMaker Network submenu controls networking using FileMaker itself. You share the database using FileMaker Server or FileMaker Pro; users log in from their own copies of FileMaker using the Open Remote command.

Figure 8.11 shows the FileMaker Network Settings dialog.

First, check that network sharing is on (refer to the radio buttons at the top of the dialog). After it is on, FileMaker shows you your TCP/IP address. Users need it if they are accessing your network from beyond your local area network.

> ### ✎ NOTE
>
> If you have a static IP address, people from anywhere on the Internet can log on using the Open Remote command and this IP address, subject to firewall settings as well as the database and privilege settings you have set. They type the address into the bottom of the Open Remote dialog using the syntax fmnet:/10.0.1.2/.
>
> Most dial-up, cable, and DSL accounts do not use static IP addresses. Contact your ISP for terms, conditions, and costs of obtaining a static IP address if you want to allow FileMaker networking access (as opposed to Instant Web Publishing access, which is discussed in step 7).

FileMaker Network Settings

FIGURE 8.11 Set FileMaker network settings.

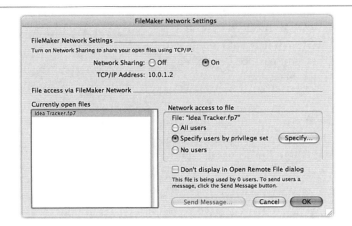

For each of the currently open files (at the lower left), you can choose the access you will allow. It can be all users, no users, or specified users by privilege set. In setting up a privilege set, you were able to set extended privileges including FileMaker networking and Instant Web Publishing. In order for someone to gain access to a database, his privilege set must allow networking and the database must allow that privilege set access. Without both sides of the equation, access is not granted.

If you choose access by privilege set, the dialog shown in Figure 8.12 opens.

FIGURE 8.12 Specify users by privilege set.

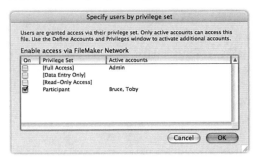

Click the check boxes next to the privilege sets that you want to allow access. If a privilege set has multiple accounts, you are providing access to all of those accounts.

The Instant Web Publishing command enables you to set up comparable access for Instant Web Publishing, as shown in Figure 8.13. Check that overall Instant Web Publishing is turned on. You are given your URL (rather than the TCP/IP address used for FileMaker networking). Setting up access privileges is the same as for FileMaker networking.

The Advanced Web Publishing options are shown in Figure 8.14. The most important option is the *port* number. By default, a web server (which is what Instant Web Publishing is) runs on port 80. You can change that port, but people who access your database will need to add the port number to the URL they use. If your URL is 10.0.1.2, access on port 80 can be obtained by typing http://10.0.1.2 into a browser. But access on another port (such as 591) requires explicitly setting the port, as in http://10.0.1.2:591.

FIGURE 8.13 Set up
Instant Web Publishing
sharing.

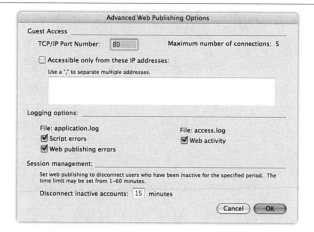

FIGURE 8.14 Set
Advanced Web Publishing
options if necessary.

 NOTE

If you have a firewall, you need to open port 5003 for FileMaker networking to work.

STEP 7 ▼
Testing Instant Web Publishing

To test Instant Web Publishing, use a browser to open the URL indicated on the Instant Web Publishing setup dialog. You can do this over the network or from your own computer. (Remember that FileMaker still must be running with the settings from the previous step.)

You first see the Instant Web Publishing home page that lists the available databases. (In the lower right of the setup dialog shown previously in Figure 8.13, you are able to hide databases from the home page.) The home page is shown in Figure 8.15.

You are prompted to enter an account name and password. Note that a full-access account (such as admin) might not have access to the database if you have not specifically enabled it as described in the previous step.

If you have not used Instant Web Publishing before, you might notice a few minor interface differences between it and FileMaker Pro itself. Figure 8.16 shows the database in a browser. The status area on the left is different from that in the desktop edition of FileMaker Pro. However, the layouts in the center of the window are rendered fairly accurately.

FIGURE 8.15   Shared databases appear on the Instant Web Publishing home page.

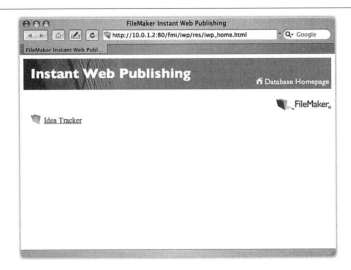

FIGURE 8.16   The Instant Web Publishing version of the database is very similar to the desktop version.

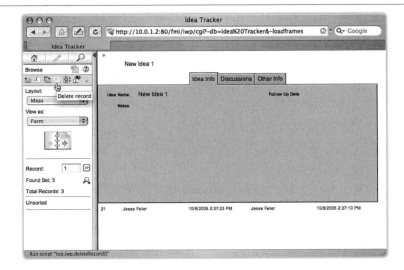

The biggest difference that you might notice is the change in the sequence of events concerning data entry. On the desktop, as you create a new record or begin to enter data in a record, that record is locked, and other people cannot access it. On the Web, the record is locked (or created if necessary) after you have entered the data; you need to click the Submit button, as shown in Figure 8.17.

There is another difference with regard to sequencing that you might also notice. With the security settings you have implemented on the desktop, an error is generated if

someone attempts to delete a record created by another user. On the Web, the sequence is reversed: The Delete Record button is disabled if the deletion is not allowed, and there is no need for an error message. Figure 8.18 shows the Delete Record button enabled at the left; you can see from the administrative information at the bottom of the window that Toby has created this record, and Toby, who is the current user, can delete it. Compare this with the record shown in Figure 8.16 that was created by someone else—and where the Delete Record button is disabled.

FIGURE 8.17   Click Submit to enter changes.

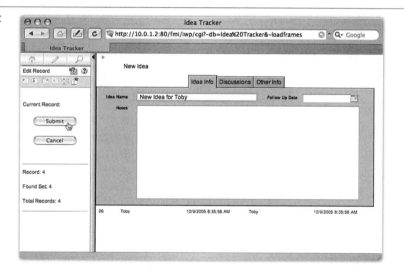

FIGURE 8.18 The Delete
Record button is only
enabled if deletion is
allowed.

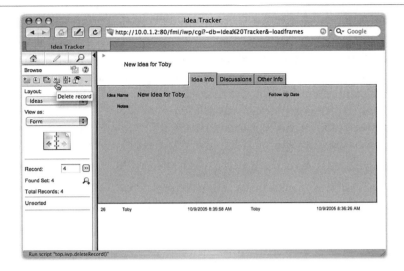

Final Thoughts

The steps you have taken in this project to reuse an existing database for another purpose and to implement security are steps that you will take many times as you implement FileMaker solutions. Both sequences require a number of simple steps to be taken, but you need to remember to do them all so your database is not partially converted or partially secure. You might want to refer to these steps in the future as you implement new databases.

The steps for Instant Web Publishing are simple, but, as with security and reuse of databases, you need to remember to take them all. In particular, remember that for networking (FileMaker networking as well as Instant Web Publishing), you need to enable networking access both from the database side and from the user side. If both sides do not allow networking, it will not work.

One final note about Instant Web Publishing: It really is simple, and the web-based database is as close as possible to the desktop version as can be. For rapid deployment of a database in a small group, nothing can beat Instant Web Publishing. It is fast and very cost-effective. Except for the one user who is hosting the database, users do not even need copies of FileMaker Pro because they can use their web browsers.

The only issues you need to address are

> ► Do you have any limitations on your ability to run a web server (which is what Instant Web Publishing is) on your network? Although many Internet service providers do not allow you to run a web server on a standard consumer account, you can run a web server on your own network in your home or office as long as people from the outside do not access it.

▶ Will you need more than five users? FileMaker Pro and FileMaker Pro Advanced are limited to five concurrent network and Instant Web Publishing users. Also, FileMaker networking with these products is limited to 125 files; Instant Web Publishing is limited to 10 files. For greater capacity, you need FileMaker Server Advanced.

CHAPTER 9: Implementing a Scheduling Solution

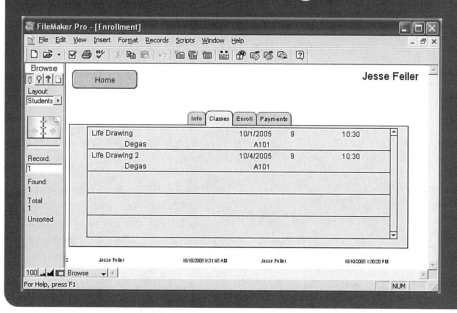

About the Project

This project has a different data structure from previous projects. It has two primary tables (Students and Classes) and they are joined together with a join table—Enrollments. This enables you to view all of the classes for each student and all of the students in a class. This type of solution applies to many other real-world situations, including almost all scheduling scenarios.

The project interface uses several layouts and a *tab control* for navigation. This chapter does not use buttons for basic FileMaker commands. See Chapter 10,"Implementing a Runtime Solution," for an example of a totally customized interface.

Prerequisites

This project relies on the Shell.fp7 table for setting up its tables.

@work resources

Please visit the publisher's website to access the following Chapter 9 files:

► Enrollment.fp7
► Shell.fp7

Planning the Project

In addition to the basic planning described in Chapter 3, "Building FileMaker Solutions," you need to consider three other issues:

▶ Planning the data rules

▶ Planning the interface

▶ Preparing to create new records with scripts and globals

Planning the Data Rules

Whether you are actually implementing a class enrollment solution or are using this design for one of its other applications, it is crucial to start by setting out the rules. These have nothing to do with FileMaker or databases and everything to do with the application itself. If you are converting a currently manual process, you are faced with the problem of deciding which existing rules will be enforced by the database and which rules will remain matters of human judgment.

Some of the issues to be addressed are

▶ Can people unenroll?

▶ If they can unenroll, are there time restrictions? (If you are using this as a scheduling solution, remember that many hotels allow you to cancel reservations but, after a certain time, there is a fee.)

▶ Can classes be cancelled? What happens to students who have enrolled? What happens to their fees?

▶ This solution provides a simple payment system. Do you want to allow partial payments? This payment system accepts payments for a student's outstanding balance. If a student takes several classes, is each one billed separately?

▶ Can someone enroll in the same class twice?

Every real-world database solution requires people to think about issues such as these.

Planning the Interface

Another critical part of the planning process is designing the interface. Here, a variety of data can be entered and displayed. There are two primary sources of data: Students and Classes. Each of these is a table, and each contains the identifying information for its own data. A join table, Enrollments, links the two. A Payments table is related to Students, and it tracks payments.

One possible interface, which is the one chosen here, will rely on three primary layouts:

▶ The Home layout opens by default when the file is opened.

▶ The Classes layout contains data for a given class. It contains a portal showing the students registered in that class.

▶ The Students layout presents data from Students and related tables. It does this with four tabs:

　▶ Info provides access to student information that is stored in Students.

- Classes contains a portal showing the classes in which a student is enrolled. The portal is based on Enrollments (the join table), but it shows data from the Classes table, which is where the basic class information is stored.

- Enroll allows you to enroll the student in a class. It contains interface elements to quickly locate the specific class to be used.

- Payments contains a portal showing that student's payments.

In order to facilitate navigation, there is a button in the upper left of all layouts to return to Home. Home has two buttons: one to go to the Students layout and the other to go to the Classes layout.

✦ TIP

By setting up the navigation rules at the beginning, you can save yourself some time. For example, in this case you always need a Home button in the upper left of each layout. Instead of cutting, pasting, and carefully positioning it, you can place it in one layout and then copy that entire layout for each successive layout.

If you display the five administrative fields at the bottom of each layout, those, too, can be placed properly and aligned/distributed in the first layout. They are copied automatically as part of the layout when you duplicate it. You will have to remember to double-click each one and reset it to the base table of each subsequent layout, but all the positioning will only have to be done once.

Preparing to Create New Records with Scripts and Globals

As your databases become more complex, you have to give some thought to the mechanics of creating new records. In a simple database (or in the basic parts of this database), creating a new record is easy: Use the New Record command and type in the data. You can and should use validation rules to check that the entered data is valid; by not allowing the rules to be overridden you can ensure that the data is valid or that the user must revert to old values or delete the record.

But what do you do when you need to create a record that is related to one or more other records (which is always the case in a join table)?

For a simple relationship, you can use the time-honored FileMaker technique of a portal that allows the creation of new records (specified in the Define Database dialog's Relationships tab). As the user types in data to fields in the blank record that is available at the bottom of the portal, FileMaker is able to automatically insert the appropriate value in the related field so the new record always preserves its relationship.

But if the relationship involves more than one field or if it is not one of equality, FileMaker cannot automatically insert the appropriate value(s), and therefore you cannot rely on this portal-based method of creating new related records.

One solution is to create the related records with a script. Such a script typically has the following structure:

1. Go to a layout based on the table to which the new record will be added.

2. Create a new record.

3. Set the first related field to the first value of the script parameter.

4. Continue with all other related fields and any other fields you want to set.

5. Go to the original layout.

The related record is created and you are back where you started. If you started in a portal, the related record is there.

For this type of script to work, you need to be able to pass in a script parameter that contains the necessary values. One or more might come from fields in the record from which you started (a student ID, for example), but others need to come from somewhere else. If there are values that a user would normally see (the amount of a payment, for example), you can create a custom dialog to ask for the values. But you need to cache them somewhere so you can pick them up and put them into the script parameter.

Also, you might need values that the user will not see. In a join table, for example, you might be using zID values for the two tables that are joined, but the user is used to seeing names, not identifying numbers.

In all of these cases, it is useful to have some global values into which you can place these values temporarily until you need them in a script.

This mechanism is used in this project for processing payments and enrollments. That is why some global values are inserted into the tables. They will be used later.

 TIP

Here is another tip you can use in any project. The Home layout need not be based on any of the data tables, so you can base it on any of the tables that you want: It normally will not display data.

But if you want, it can contain data. The Home layout is the right place to display preferences and other global data. You can create a Preferences table and store global information in it to display in the Home layout. Alternatively, you can store multiple records of information and preferences and automatically retrieve it based on the current user's name.

Project: Class Enrollment

We'll be creating the Class Enrollment solution in 11 easy steps:

STEPS ▼

1. Getting started
2. Creating the fields for the Students table
3. Creating the fields for the Classes table
4. Creating the fields for the Enrollments table
5. Creating the fields for the Payments table
6. Setting up the relationships
7. Building the Home layout and navigation script
8. Building the Classes layout
9. Building the Students layout
10. Implementing the Enroll process
11. Implementing the Payment process

Getting Started

This project consists of a single database file with four tables in it:

- ▶ Students
- ▶ Classes
- ▶ Enrollments
- ▶ Payments

The Enrollments table is the join table that joins Students to Classes in a many-to-many relationship. The Payments table is related to the Students table in a many-to-one relationship (one student may make many payments). The total amount due is stored in a calculation field in the Students table along with the total amount paid. This puts all of a student's vital information in one place.

To get started, create a new database file and populate it with these four tables. In each table, make certain that you have the five administrative fields that have been used in every project in this book. Those fields are automatically filled in by FileMaker, so they take no extra time and almost no extra space. Their presence makes relationships easy to build because you know that every record will have a zID field. Also, you know that you can use the Count function to count the number of related records by counting

the number of values in the related zID field: There is one such value for every record.

Depending on which version of FileMaker Pro you have and how you choose to work, there are a number of ways of building this database file with its four tables and each table's five default fields:

- ▶ If you have FileMaker Pro 8 Advanced, you can copy Shell.fp7 and rename it Enrollment.fp7. Open it and rename the Shell table Enrollments. Then use the Copy and Paste commands in the table pane of the Define Database dialog to make copies. Rename the copies Students, Classes, and Payments.

- ▶ If you do not have FileMaker Pro 8 Advanced or if you have FileMaker Pro 7, copy Shell.fp7 and rename the Shell table as described previously. Then manually add three tables and populate them with the required fields.

- ▶ Start from a blank database and create all four tables and each table's five default fields.

Whatever method you choose, the Relationships tab of the Define Database dialog should look like Figure 9.1 (allowing for changes in spacing). If it does not, adjust the tables, names, or whatever needs changing.

FIGURE 9.1   Create the
Enrollment database file
with four tables and their
default fields.

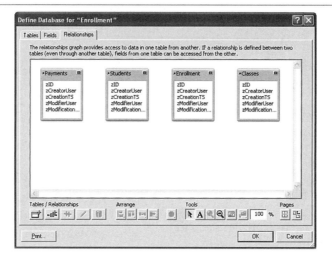

STEP 2 ▼
Creating the Fields for the Students Table

The Students table needs the following fields, shown in Figure 9.2, in addition to the five administrative fields (they will not be referenced again because they are used in every table):

 TIP

As these fields are created, make certain that you properly set their data types. Any field that contains a number should be identified as a number, dates as dates, and so forth. This enables you to use FileMaker's built-in editing and data checking. Also indicate which fields are required and where duplicates are or are not allowed. In that regard, be careful about not boxing yourself into a corner. People sometimes do have duplicate names, and you can use other information (address, for example) to distinguish among them. Forcing users to distort names (by using or even inventing middle initials) can cause problems. Enforce rules that are realistic.

▶ **First Name and Last Name**—These need to be separate fields so you can sort them in a normal order (last name, first name) but present them in a standard order (first name, last name). The Last Name field is required to be non-blank.

▶ **Address**—This is a single field in this project. You probably want to make it into a number of fields for street address, city, state or province, postal code, telephone, and so forth. You might want other information for the student as well. All of that information is handled the same as the address is handled, so it is not included here.

▶ **Notes**—This is space for comments about a student.

FIGURE 9.2   **Create the fields for the** Students **table.**

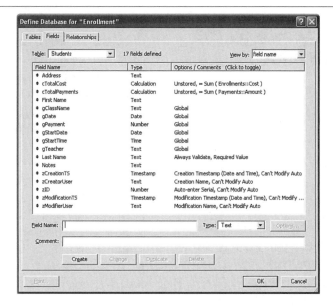

- ▸ **Global fields**—Several global fields are used to assist in looking up classes in the Enroll tab. These fields are used in a relationship and will be explained in step 6: gStartDate, gStartTime, gClassName, gTeacher. Remember that these are globals and must be marked as globals in the Storage tab of the Options button's dialog in the Fields tab in the Define Database dialog; their naming adheres to the convention that globals are identified by their names. Two other global fields, gPayment and gDate, are used to process payments, as described in step 11.

- ▸ **Calculation fields**—Two calculation fields are used to calculate the sum of payments made and amounts due. These are mentioned here for completion, but they must be created after the relationships are built in step 6.

STEP 3 ▼
Creating the Fields for the Classes Table

The fields for Classes are as follows:

- ▸ **Class Name**—This must be non-blank.

- ▸ **Teacher**—In a more complex implementation, there would be a separate Teachers table from which you would choose a teacher's name.

- ▸ **Start Date**

- ▸ **Start Time**

- ▸ **End Time**

- ▸ **Location**

- ▸ **Cost**

- ▸ **Notes**

Creating the Fields for the Enrollments Table

The Enrollments table is a common join table. The fields are

▸ **Student ID and Class ID**—These are related to the zID fields in Students and Classes to actually perform the join.

▸ **Cost**—This is looked up from Classes, but it can be modified here. This allows you to build in logic beyond that shown in this project to account for scholarships, discounts, and the like. If you want to add those features, you need to be able to use a per-enrollment field such as this. This field cannot be created until the relationships are built in step 6.

▸ **Notes**

Creating the Fields for the Payments Table

Finally, the Payments table has three fairly obvious fields:

▸ Amount

▸ Date

▸ Notes

You can use the Notes field to record a check number or other identifying data. You also need a Date field in addition to the zCreationTS and zModificationTS fields. Those fields are filled in automatically by FileMaker based on the time of record creation or modification. Sometimes the date of a payment is different—data might be entered manually on a receipt and then entered into the computer the next day or month. The date might also be later than the creation or modification date of the record; this could occur if the student presents a post-dated check when enrolling in a course in personal financial management.

Setting Up the Relationships

With all of the fields set up (except those that depend on relationships and that will be set up in this step), you can easily create the relationships. There are three primary relationships:

▸ zID in Students is related to Student ID in Payments

▸ zID in Students is related to Student ID in Enrollments

▸ zID in Classes is related to Class ID in Enrollments

A relationship is also used in the Enroll portal to quickly identify a class in which to enroll a student. For now, simply create the relationship; it will be explained as that interface is built. Create a new table occur-rence based on `Classes`; name it `Classes Lookup`. Now, create a relationship from `Class Name` in `Classes` to `gClassName` in `Students` (it does not matter in which direction the relationship is drawn). Double-click the relationship icon in the middle of the relationship to open the Relationship dialog shown in Figure 9.3. Add the addi-tional relationship for `gStartDate`, `gStartTime`, and `gTeacher` as shown in the figure.

After you have established the relationships, you can now create the three fields mentioned previously:

▶ In `Students`, create calculations based on the sum of `Payments::Amount` and `Enrollments::Amount`. These fields are shown in Figure 9.2.

▶ In `Enrollments`, add the field `Cost` and its lookup from `Classes::Cost`.

The database graph should now look like the illustration in Figure 9.4.

FIGURE 9.3 **Create the multiple relationship to** `Classes Lookup`.

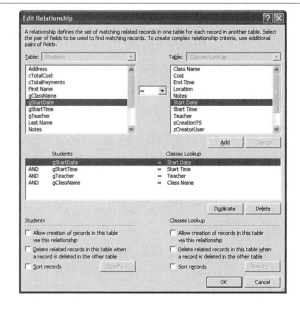

FIGURE 9.4 **The database fields and relationships are complete.**

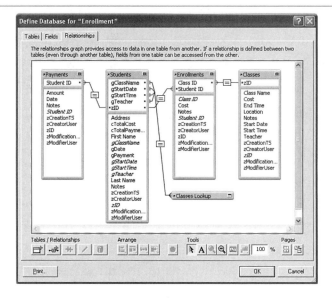

STEP 7 ▼
Building the Home Layout and Navigation Script

The Home layout is the simplest layout. If you decide to implement a `Preferences` table, the layout is based on that table. Otherwise, it does not matter what table it is based on because it will not display data. You can place a logo or title text on this layout as you see fit. It needs two buttons: One goes to the Students layout and the other goes to the Classes layout.

A navigation script handles this navigation and the other major navigation needs of buttons in the solution. The basic script is shown in Figure 9.5. The logic is that you pass in a script parameter. Based on its value, the script determines to which layout

to go. Then it resizes the window to fit the layout. Note the `else` clause: If there is no script parameter, the script goes to the Home layout. You cannot complete the script yet because layouts must exist before you can add Go To Layout script steps for them, but the `else` requires no script parameter and it requires the Home layout on which you are now working. So you can start building the script.

Draw a button and label it Students. Attach the script to it even though it will not work yet. Duplicate the button and rename it Classes. The script is attached to it as well. Now place the buttons as you want on the layout. It looks something like Figure 9.6. Duplicating the button after the script is attached automatically makes it the same size and you do not have to worry about attaching the script.

FIGURE 9.5   Build a
navigation script.

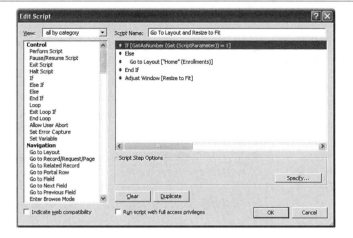

FIGURE 9.6   The Home
layout is complete.

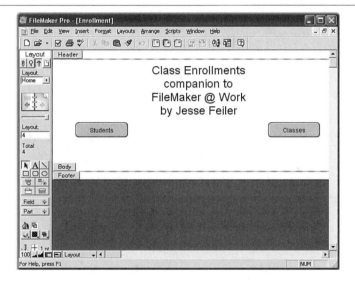

STEP 8 ▼
Building the Classes Layout

This is the simpler of the two main layouts, so it is a good place to start. First, copy one of the buttons from the Home layout. Now, create a new layout based on the Classes table. Place the button in the upper left of the header and rename it Home.

Place the five administrative fields along the bottom in the footer and resize them to a small font size. Align their tops or bottoms and distribute the space. After you are happy with this layout, duplicate it. Use Layout Setup to change its base table to Students and double-click the five fields at the bottom to reassign them to fields with the same names in the Students table, not the Classes table.

You now have two identical layouts, one based on Classes and one on Students. One is shown in Figure 9.7.

The Home button in the Classes and Students layouts should work now, returning you to the Home layout. Test it.

You can complete the script for the moment. Add to it as shown in Figure 9.8.

Return to the Home layout and modify the buttons to include the appropriate script parameter on each one (1 for the Classes layout and 2 for the Students layout in this example) as shown in Figure 9.9.

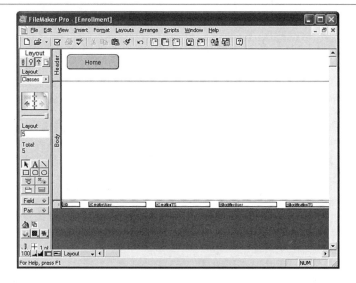

FIGURE 9.7   The Classes and Students layouts are set up and ready for customization.

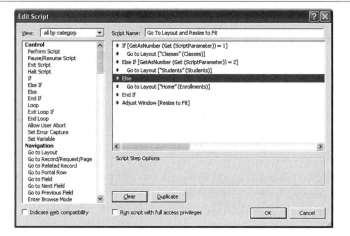

FIGURE 9.8   Complete the navigation script.

FIGURE 9.9   Add the script parameter to the buttons on the Home layout.

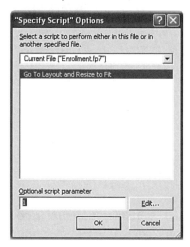

FIGURE 9.9   Add the script parameter to the buttons on the Home layout.

The navigation mechanism is now complete. Test it. You can add If elements to the script as you add more layouts to the solution. Note that this mechanism means that every navigation button has the same script attached to it. If you want to keep a log of what people are doing or if you want to add some kind of standard navigation action (such as resizing the window), you only have to make those changes in one place.

In the Classes layout, you can easily complete your work. Place the fields of the Classes layout in the center of the layout as you see fit. Remember that Cost is a number: Format it using the Number command in the Format menu. Likewise, format the dates and times appropriately. If you want, you can add the new drop-down calendar to the Start Date field in the Field/Control Setup command of the Format menu.

A common convention is to display the name of an entity in a non-editable field at the top of a layout. Here, the class name is set as a *merge field* in large type. You enter and modify the class name in the body of the layout, and it is shown for reference at the top.

The completed layout is shown in Figure 9.10.

FIGURE 9.10   The Classes layout is complete.

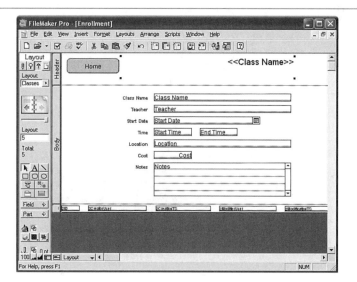

STEP 9 ▼
Building the Students Layout

The Students layout is the most complex, but its complexity is kept under control by using a tab control. Starting from the copy of the basic Classes layout that is now based on the Students layout (refer to Figure 9.7), use the Insert Merge Field command to insert the First Name and Last Name fields in the upper right of the layout, in the same way that you put the class name in the upper right of the Classes layout. Then, in the body of the layout, draw a large tab control with four tabs:

- ▶ Info
- ▶ Classes
- ▶ Enroll
- ▶ Payments

Figure 9.11 shows the layout at this point.

The Info tab displays the basic information for the student as shown in Figure 9.12. Its fields are

- ▶ First Name
- ▶ Last Name
- ▶ Address
- ▶ Notes
- ▶ The two calculation fields, cTotalCost and cTotalPayments

If you have added additional information to the table, you can display it here (telephone number, email address, and so forth). If there is a lot of additional information, you can split it into two tabs: double-click the tab control's background or choose Tab Control Setup from the Format menu to add one or more tabs, rename tabs, and reorder them.

FIGURE 9.11 Draw a tab control in the Students layout.

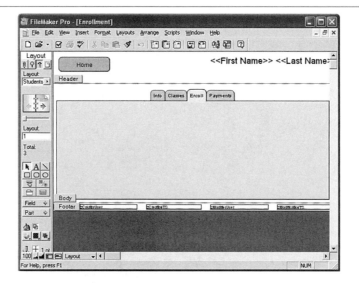

FIGURE 9.12 Complete the Info tab.

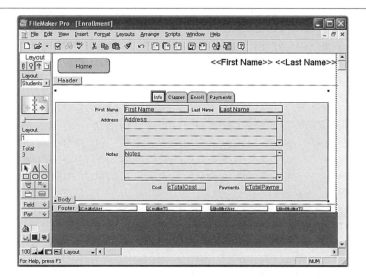

The Classes tab is very simple. It consists of a portal onto the Classes table with information for this student's classes. You can draw the portal in the center of the tab control's Classes tab (the tabs work in layout mode to switch from one to another); when prompted for the fields to display, choose the ones you want. Figure 9.13 shows the tab with the completed portal in it. Note that the portal has been drawn so two rows of text can be contained in each row. After FileMaker has placed the fields in the portal, you can rearrange them as you see fit. You should also set their behavior so you cannot enter data into them in Browse mode.

FIGURE 9.13 The Classes tab displays classes for a single student.

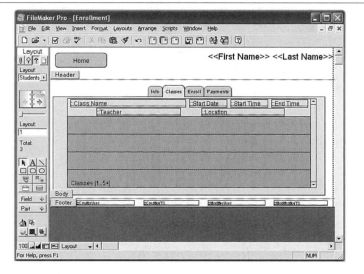

Skip over the Enroll tab to complete the Payments tab. It contains a portal onto Payments; the fields to be displayed are Date, Amount, and Notes. The fields in the portal should be non-entry fields in Browse mode.

Leave some space below the portal at the bottom of the Payments tab for a button and two fields to be used in entering a payment.

STEP 10 ▼
Implementing the Enroll Process

Along the way, you have built a spare relationship (Classes Lookup) and created some globals that are involved with it. Now you will see how it can all pay off in easily implementing enrollment.

First, to prepare the way, use the solution as it stands to enter some students and some classes if you have not done so yet.

Now, go to the Enroll tab in the Students layout and implement the enrollment process. What you will be doing is creating an interface to allow the user to select the class in which the student will be enrolled. The completed Enroll tab is shown in Figure 9.14.

At the top of the tab, four fields set the four global values that are used in the Classes Lookup relationship. The fields in the center of the tab are non-editable and provide the details of the class.

To implement those four fields for the globals, you need to do some preparatory work. Create two value lists from the values in the Class Name and Teacher fields in the Classes layout. Then, create fields in this layout for gClassName and gTeacher. Use the Field/Control Setup command in the Format menu to make these fields drop-down menus that use these new value lists.

FIGURE 9.14 **The Enroll tab enables you to easily enroll a student in a class.**

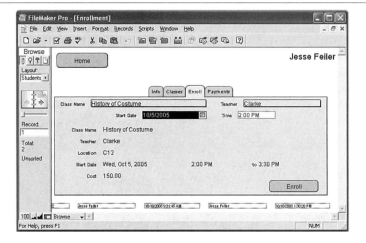

FIGURE 9.14 **The Enroll tab enables you to easily enroll a student in a class.**

Format the gStartDate and gStartTime fields appropriate for dates and times. Also, for gStartDate, set the field type to Drop-down Calendar.

Then, add the fields to the rest of this tab (mark them as non-entry fields in Browse mode). Note that these fields are from the Classes Lookup table, not from Classes. You are using Classes Lookup because you want to get to the class identified by those four global fields. The data is displayed so the user can verify that this is the right class; what you want is the Classes Lookup::zID field in order to construct the join table.

Next you need a script to create a new record in the Enrollments table. The script follows the structure described at the beginning of this chapter. It is shown in Figure 9.15.

The last step is to create the Enroll button. Attach the Enroll script shown in Figure 9.15 to it, and set the script parameter to the three needed values:

```
Students::zID & ¶ &
Classes Lookup::zID & ¶ &
Classes Lookup::Cost
```

Go back into Browse mode and try it. When you click Enroll, the student is enrolled in the class. Click the Classes tab to see the list of classes for that student and this class is there. Furthermore, on the Info tab, you see the total cost of classes, updated with this class's cost.

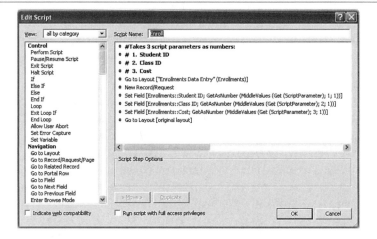

FIGURE 9.15 **Write a script to create a record in the** Enrollments **join table.**

STEP 11 ▼
Implementing the Payment Process

The Payment process is almost the same as the Enroll process, but it is simpler because you do not have to look up a class identifier and there is no join table. There is a simple one-to-many relationship from the student to payments.

You need a script that is similar to the Enroll script to process payments. Three values are passed in: the student ID, the payment amount, and the date. This means that the third Set Fields line needs to recieve the third value of the script parameter as a date, not as a number as it does in the Enroll script:

```
GetAsDate (MiddleValues
  (Get (ScriptParameter), 3, 1))
```

After the script is created, you can go to the Payments tab of the Students layout. When you created the portal, you left some space at the bottom of the tab. (If you did not, rearrange things.) In that space, place two fields: gDate and gPayment. These are the globals that you created to use in implementing payments. Then, create a Pay button using the new script; for a script parameter, pass in the zID of the Students record, the payment amount, and the date:

```
Students::zID & ¶ &
Students::gPayment & ¶ &
Students::gDate
```

The completed Payments tab is shown in Figure 9.16.

Test it. You should see payments register in the portal; you should also see the updated balance paid on the Info tab.

FIGURE 9.16   The
Payments tab is complete.

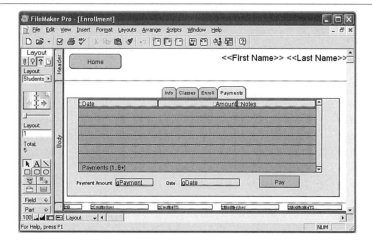

You could use the global fields in the Pay script rather than passing them in as parameters. The advantage of passing them in as parameters is that it is only a few keystrokes of extra work here, and it allows you to use the script in another context in which the global fields might not be available.

Also, in comparing enrollment with payments, everything is done on one tab for payments. For enrollments, you need two tabs: one to display the portal and the other to display the interface to locate a class. This is simply a reflection of the amount of space needed for the interface elements.

Final Thoughts

Planning the database fields and relationships might seem like a lot of effort, but, in fact, it is the bulk of the project. When planned properly, you will have all of the pieces in place to quickly implement functionality. Notice how quickly it all came together after you drew the Enroll and Pay buttons. All of the data and relationships were there and they just worked.

The more work you can push into the database and its schema and out of your scripts, the better off you are. This project has only three very short scripts, and they all do the same sort of thing—collect data and place it into a new record or navigate from one layout to another. In both cases, the generalized scripts are modified with script parameters so they can be extended and reused.

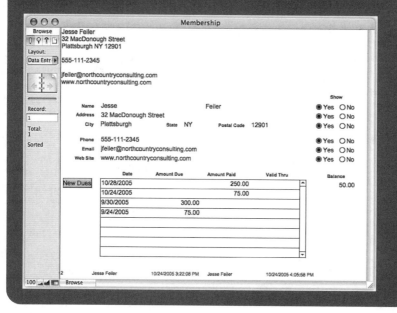

About the Project

This project keeps track of organization membership and demonstrates customized menu sets, data hiding, custom security privileges, and runtime solutions. It runs using FileMaker Pro or the runtime solution.

Prerequisites

This project relies on the Shell.fp7 table. It is created using FileMaker Pro Advanced.

@work resources

Please visit the publisher's website to access the following Chapter 10 files:

- ▶ **Membership.fp7**
- ▶ **Shell.fp7**
- ▶ **Runtime Solution for Mac OS X** (folder)
- ▶ **Runtime Solution for Windows** (folder)

Use the account name Manager with a blank password to open the runtime solutions.

...ing the Project

...cause FileMaker makes it so easy to modify databases and solutions, it is generally possible to start from a general idea of what you want and experiment with it, gradually evolving the solution you develop. Planning ahead remains essential for large-scale projects on fixed schedules, but often you can put up a solution on an informal basis without a great deal of planning. As you have seen in the other projects in this book, much of the up-front planning that you need to do is centered on what the project will actually do—the business aspects, not the database aspects.

Some things really do require advance planning, however. It is very difficult to retrofit security and version control to a project (this applies to everything from a FileMaker solution to an operating system).

This project stores two types of data: name and address information and payment information. As implemented, it has two sets of privileges. One set provides access to everything, and the other set provides view-only guest access. It also implements a system that allows the hiding of certain data.

When building your own project or modifying this one, you will need to decide what types of data access you will allow to what groups of people. Although this can be retrofitted to a certain extent, if you customize the privileges in FileMaker, you will need to

make certain that your tables and layouts are set up in such a way that you can implement the security you need. For that reason, the security requirements that might seem like the last step in a project should really be the first.

Project: Membership List

We'll be creating the Membership List solution in 12 easy steps:

STEPS ▼

1. Getting started
2. Adding basic fields to the Membership table
3. Implementing data hiding
4. Adding basic fields to the Dues table
5. Creating the Membership/Dues relationship and calculating the balance
6. Creating a data entry layout
7. Adding a New Dues script and button
8. Creating the Membership List layout
9. Creating custom menu sets
10. Setting accounts and privileges
11. Finishing security
12. Creating the runtime solution

STEP 1 ▼
Getting Started

The project consists of a single database file (Membership) that contains two tables: Membership and Dues. Start by creating those tables and filling them with the five administrative fields that are auto-entered with creator and modifier names, timestamps, and a unique serial number. You can build on the Shell.fp7 file or, if you are using FileMaker Pro Advanced, you can import the table from Shell.fp7 into a new database file.

STEP 2 ▼
Adding Basic Fields to the Membership Table

This table contains the basic contact information for members. Start by creating those fields:

- ▶ First Name
- ▶ Last Name
- ▶ Address
- ▶ City
- ▶ State
- ▶ Postal Code
- ▶ Phone
- ▶ Email
- ▶ Web Site

All of them are text fields.

STEP 3 ▼
Implementing Data Hiding

Data hiding is implemented using calculations. For each field that can be hidden, there are actually three fields in the database:

- ▶ There is a field that contains the data, and it can be modified and viewed by people with appropriate security privileges.

- ▶ There is a field that contains the value Yes or No to indicate whether the data should be displayed. This field is displayed as two radio buttons.

- ▶ Finally, there is a calculation field. If the radio button is set to Yes, it displays the value from the underlying field; otherwise it displays a blank. Like all calculation fields, it is not modifiable. For people with limited privileges, only this field is visible.

To implement the controlling field, create fields such as NameVisible, AddressVisible, and so forth. Set the auto-enter option to whatever default you want: In this case, the default is Yes so that the data is visible. Figure 10.1 shows the auto-enter option.

FIGURE 10.1   Set the auto-enter option for the controlling fields.

A one-to-one relationship doesn't need to exist between the controlling fields and the other fields. In this project, City, State, and Postal Code are controlled by a single field—CSPVisible. In addition, NameVisible controls the combination of First Name and Last Name.

Next, implement the calculation fields. Using the standard practice of naming calculation fields with a lower-case c, these have names such as cName, cAddress, and so forth. The single line of code for the calculation is of the form shown here:

```
If ( NameVisible = "Yes" ;
  First Name & " "  & Last Name;
  "")
```

Figure 10.2 shows the completed calculation. Remember to set the calculation result type in the lower left of the dialog to Text.

FIGURE 10.2   Create the calculations.

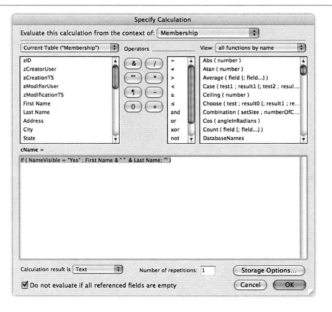

Figure 10.3 shows the fields in the Membership table as they should be at this point. They are shown in creation order so they follow the steps in this chapter.

FIGURE 10.3   **Finish the Membership fields.**

STEP 4 ▼
Adding Basic Fields to the Dues Table

In addition to the standard five administrative fields, you need fields to track the dues. Remember to use the most specific field types possible: The solution will work if Amount Due is a text field, but it is a number and should be a number field. Here are the fields that you need to add to the Dues table:

▶ Date

▶ Amount Due

▶ Amount Paid

▶ Valid Thru Date

▶ Notes

There are several ways of implementing this type of table, and it is worth considering some alternatives. In this structure, you are able to specify both the amount due and the amount paid. This can reflect a billing process with the bill generated on a certain date (and a database record reflecting that) and with a payment made on that or another date (and a separate database record reflecting that transaction).

Another structure would add a field to indicate the transaction type (`Bill` or `Payment`, for example) and use a single `Amount` field. For dues that are billed relatively infrequently, this structure works well. If you are tracking more frequent or more extensive charges, your table needs to reflect which item has been paid, and you need to create a relationship between the payment and the bill. You can do this using the self-join structure that has been described previously.

Note, too, that there is a `Valid Thru Date` field that can be used to indicate when the next payment is due. It is in the database as an indication of one of the directions in which you can go to expand the project; it is not used in this version, however.

The `Date` field uses an auto-enter calculation to set the date as shown in Figure 10.4.

FIGURE 10.4   Auto-enter the date.

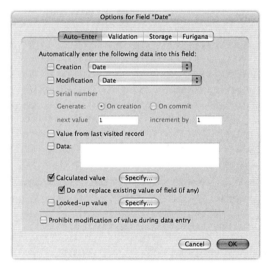

The calculation consists of this line:

```
Get ( CurrentDate )
```

Finally, you need to create a relationship between the `Dues` records and the `Membership` records. To do so, you need a `MemberID` field; it is a number, and it is used to match a `zID` field in `Membership`.

The completed table is shown in Figure 10.5.

STEP 5 ▼
Creating the Membership/Dues Relationship and Calculating the Balance

The penultimate step in building the database is to create the relationship between the `MemberID` field in `Dues` and the `zID` field in `Membership`, as shown in Figure 10.6.

After you have created the relationship, you can finish the database by creating a calculation in the `Membership` table that reflects the current balance of a member's various `Dues` records. The calculation uses the `Sum` function:

```
Sum ( Dues::Amount Due )
  - Sum ( Dues::Amount Paid )
```

The result is a number, and its name is `cBalance`.

FIGURE 10.5   Finish the
Dues **fields**.

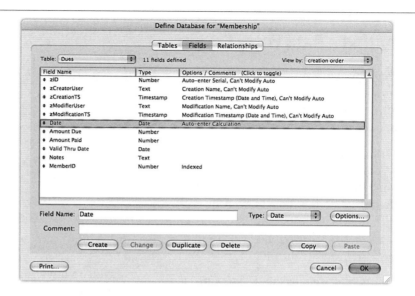

FIGURE 10.6   **Create the**
relationship.

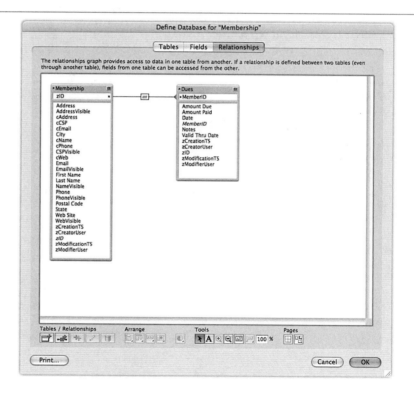

STEP 6 ▼
Creating a Data Entry Layout

As you create tables and fields, FileMaker creates default layouts for you. You can modify them or start from scratch with a blank layout to build the layouts you need.

This project has three layouts. The Data Entry layout is based on the Membership table. It displays all of the fields from that table (including the radio button controls); it also contains a portal into Dues to show the Dues records for a given member. The completed layout is shown in Figure 10.7.

In addition, a Membership List layout contains the calculated fields from Membership; it is normally shown in List view, and it has a *custom menu set*. A Dues layout is used for a script that adds Dues records and

can be expanded as you see fit. For now, the focus is on Data Entry.

In Layout mode, create a new layout using the New Layout/Report command in the Layouts menu. It should be named Data Entry, and it should be based on the Membership table. When given a choice of default layouts, choose a blank layout. Add all of the fields except the calculation fields (such as cName) from Membership to the layout.

The calculation fields show the visible information that is controlled by the radio buttons, such as NameVisible. Because it is possible to have various combinations of shown and hidden fields, it is best to use merge fields to display this data at the top of the layout. This way the data that is blank will not take up space.

FIGURE 10.7   Create a data entry layout.

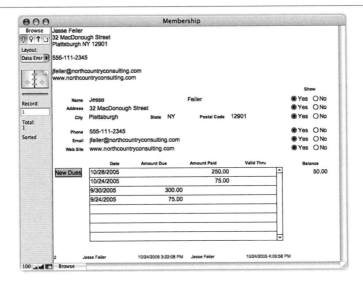

When you are preparing a report for printing, you can use the Sliding/Printing dialog to close up data, but that is only available in Preview mode. Merge fields are a much easier way of setting up this functionality.

Figure 10.8 shows the layout at this step.

FIGURE 10.8   **Build the Data Entry layout in Layout mode.**

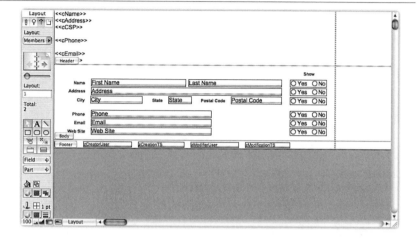

Next, enlarge the body of the layout so it is big enough to add a portal. Draw the portal with the Portal tool from the status area.

The Portal Setup dialog opens as shown in Figure 10.9.

FIGURE 10.9   **Set up the Dues portal.**

There is only one table related to Membership, so the default value for related records (Dues) is correct. You want a vertical scroll bar in the

portal and to sort the records by date, so click the Sort Portal Records check box.

After you click the Specify button next to the Sort Portal Records check box, choose to sort the records in reverse chronological order, as shown in Figure 10.10.

FIGURE 10.10   **Sort the portal records.**

In the next dialog, shown in Figure 10.11, choose the fields to display in the portal. As you can see, only four fields are needed: Date, Amount Due, Amount Paid, and Valid Thru Date.

This is a good time to check the formatting of the various fields. Numeric fields look best when they are right-aligned. The layout should resemble Figure 10.12.

The only field remaining to be used is the cBalance field. Add it to the right of the portal along with a title. FileMaker makes certain that the calculation is properly updated to reflect the records shown in the Dues portal.

FIGURE 10.11   Add fields to the portal.

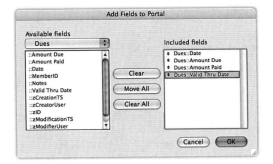

FIGURE 10.12   The Data Entry layout is taking shape with the Dues portal.

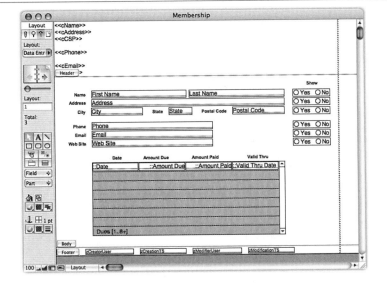

STEP 7 ▼
Adding a New Dues Script and Button

The relationship between Membership and Dues is a simple equijoin, so it is possible to use the long-standing FileMaker practice of allowing people to enter new data in a blank row that is always available at the bottom of the portal. This interface technique, however, is not available for relationships that are not equijoins or that involve more than one set of fields. Adding a button next to a portal allows you to create a consistent user experience for yourself and your users when it comes to adding related records. For this reason, it is a good idea to take the slight

extra time involved in creating a button and the script that goes with it.

Start with the script. It is called New Dues and creates the related record and explicitly sets the MemberID field using a parameter that is passed in.

Before proceeding, check that you have a Dues layout in the database file. If you have followed the steps so far, FileMaker has built a default Dues layout for you. If it is missing, create a new layout called Dues that is based on the Dues table. That is sufficient, but you probably want to add all of the Dues fields to the layout in case you need to use it for debugging.

The script is shown in Figure 10.13.

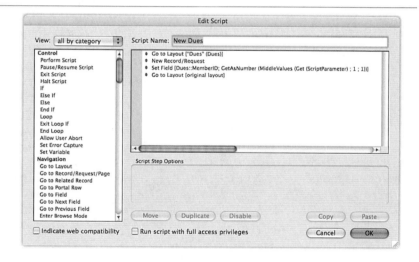

FIGURE 10.13   Create a New Dues script.

This script is similar to other scripts you have seen in other projects. It is designed to be expanded, which is why it uses the MiddleValues function to split the script parameter into its component pieces. Right

now, there is only one component piece—the membership ID—but this code allows you to add other components as the need arises.

Finally, draw a New Dues button to the left of the portal and attach the script to it.

Remember to set the script parameter to the zID field of the Membership table as shown in Figure 10.14.

FIGURE 10.14   Attach the script to a New Dues button.

The Data Entry layout is now complete. Experiment with the radio buttons that show and hide fields; add new Dues records. Watch how FileMaker automatically updates the balance and handles the spacing issues at the top as data is shown and hidden.

STEP 8 ▼

Creating the Membership List Layout

This is a simple step. In Layout mode, choose New Layout/Report from the Layouts menu and allow it to step you through the process of creating a new layout called Membership List that is based on Membership. Create it as a blank layout, and then paste the calculation fields from the header of Data Entry into the body of Membership List.

Create a script as shown in Figure 10.15 to display the layout. You should be aware of one trick to this script. The script displays the data in List view, and it sorts the data by name. The field that is uses to sort the data is cName, not First Name and Last Name. The reason is that if the name is to be hidden (using NameVisible) it should be totally hidden. Sorting on the actual name fields might allow the supposedly hidden name data to be identified by the order of the other record information in the list.

FIGURE 10.15   Create a Membership List script.

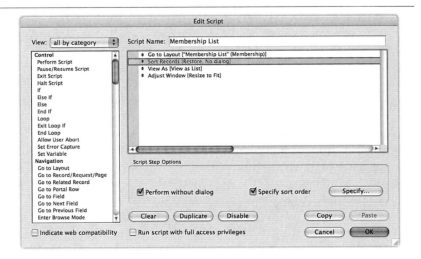

STEP 9 ▼
Creating Custom Menu Sets

Until FileMaker Pro 8, you could not do much with the menus in FileMaker. Several FileMaker-provided sets of menus allowed varying degrees of access, but that was it. Now you have the ability to create *custom menus*; you combine them into menu sets, and you can now associate those menu sets with individual layouts.

In this step, you create a new menu set for guest access to the database. It is severely limited in the commands that it offers.

You need FileMaker Pro Advanced to create those custom menus and menu sets. The Layout Setup dialog shown in Figure 10.16 enables you to manage this process.

FIGURE 10.16   Use the Layout Setup dialog to manage custom menu sets.

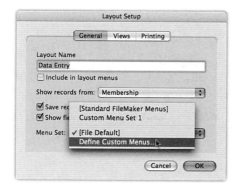

When you begin to create custom menu sets from the Layout Setup dialog, the Define Custom Menus dialog shown in Figure 10.17 opens. This is the same interface used in FileMaker for features such as privileges. FileMaker-defined menu sets are titled with square brackets, and you can create your own menu sets with titles you provide that are not enclosed in square brackets. Note at the bottom of the dialog that you can set a default menu set for all the tables and layouts in a file; in addition, you can still customize each layout in the Layout Setup dialog to use its own menu set.

FIGURE 10.17   **Create and edit menu sets.**

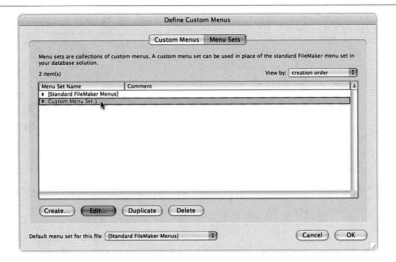

When you create or edit a menu set, the Edit Menu Set dialog shown in Figure 10.18 opens. If you had any doubt about the previous note regarding the confusion you can create by modifying menus and menu sets, this dialog should convince you. You can do almost anything here.

FIGURE 10.18   **Edit a menu set.**

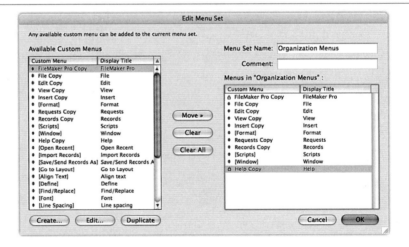

At the upper right is the name of the menu set. There is room for a comment, and you should provide one. The menus in the menu set are shown in the list at the right of the dialog. You can rearrange the menus except for the menus that are marked by padlocks: FileMaker requires that they be in specific locations.

The custom menus are shown at the left. You can create and edit them using the Edit Custom Menu dialog shown in Figure 10.19. It contains all the tools you need to modify the menus and their commands.

For the Membership List project, the task at hand is simple. The Guest Menus menu set consists of the two default FileMaker menus as well as the FileMaker-provided Scripts and Window menus. Delete the others so the Guest Menus menu set appears as it does in Figure 10.20.

FIGURE 10.19 **Edit custom menus.**

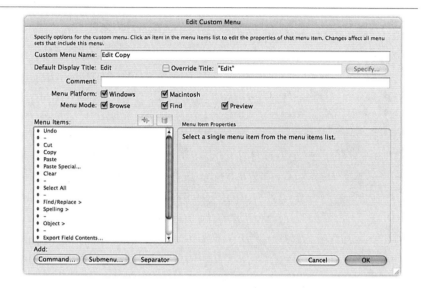

FIGURE 10.20 **Delete unneeded menus.**

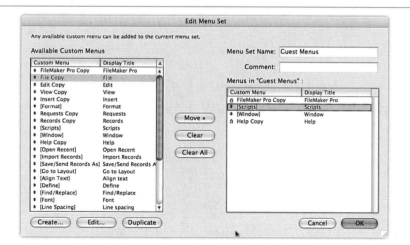

Remember that when you create scripts, you can choose whether they appear in the Scripts menu, so that level of control is also available to you (and is used in this project).

Finish up by attaching the Guest Menus menu set to the Membership List layout using the Layout Setup dialog as shown in Figure 10.21. When you return to Browse mode, you can confirm that the menus change as you move from Membership List to Data Entry.

FIGURE 10.21 Attach the Guest Menus menu set to the Membership List layout.

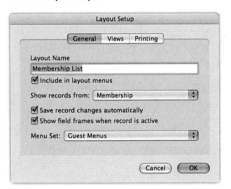

STEP 10 ▼
Setting Accounts and Privileges

As you did with Idea Tracker in Chapter 8, "Creating a Secure Shared Database," you now need to set up accounts and privileges. A new full-access account, Manager, is created along with a very limited Guest account that uses the customized Guest Access *privilege set* shown in Figure 10.22. The process is the same as that used in Chapter 8, so it is not repeated here.

STEP 11 ▼
Finishing Security

You need to tie up a few loose ends in order to complete the security implementation. One important consideration is that you need to make certain that users get to the right layout when they log in. If you have set up the custom privileges to deny access to Data Entry for guest users, you need to open the database file in Membership List in order to avoid an error.

FIGURE 10.22 Create a Guest Access privilege set.

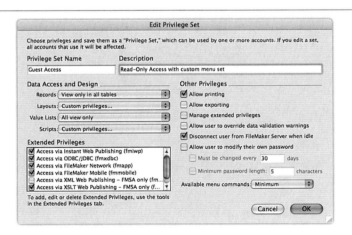

CHAPTER 10: Implementing a Runtime Solution

If you always open the database file using Membership List, however, you will be caught up in the custom menu set attached to it. There is no way for a user to get to the Data Entry layout from there.

The solution is to write a startup script to be run when the file is opened (set this from the File Options dialog in the File menu after you have created the script). It checks the privilege set that is in effect and chooses which layout to go to, as shown in Figure 10.23.

You will note that the script checks the privilege set name, not the user name. This is because you want to control matters from the privilege set, not from the individual user.

Double-check that all of the other security settings are correct. Remove scripts from the Scripts menu if they should not be visible using ScriptMaker. Likewise, remove layouts that should not be visible from the Layout menus using the Set Layout Order command in the Layouts menu in Layout mode. (If you are using a privilege set to restrict access to layouts, which is what is done in this project, you do not have to worry about removing layouts. FileMaker does it for you at runtime.)

FIGURE 10.23 Use a startup script to choose the right layout.

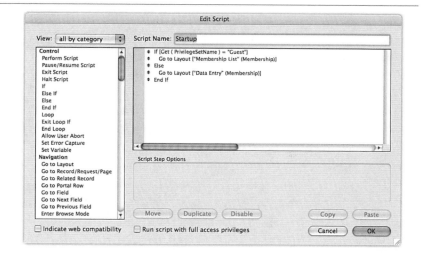

STEP 12 ▼
Creating the Runtime Solution

Test the solution to make certain that it works as you want it to. Try it with all of the accounts you have set up. When you are satisfied that it is working correctly, create the *runtime solution*.

 NOTE

The runtime solution has all of the files necessary to run it on either Mac OS X or Windows. FileMaker creates the runtime solution for the platform on which you are running.

Start by closing the database. In FileMaker Pro Advanced, choose Developer Utilities from the Tools menu. That opens the dialog shown in Figure 10.24.

A great deal of customization is available here, but for this project, the most basic settings are sufficient. (In fact, for a great many runtime solutions, these settings are sufficient.)

Add the Membership.fp7 database file to the solution using the Add button at the upper right of the dialog. You do not have to worry about setting the primary file because there is only one file, and it is primary.

Click the Specify button to set up a folder in which all of the project files will be stored.

Finally, specify the solution options as shown in Figure 10.25. Here is where you can customize the closing splash screen and make other changes. You only need to choose the Create Runtime Solution Application(s) option.

The runtime solution is created. Test it to make certain that it works as you expect it to, and then distribute it to the people who will use it. (In your testing, remember that runtime solutions do not support networking, so do not consider that a bug.)

FIGURE 10.24 Create the runtime solution.

FIGURE 10.25 Specify the solution options.

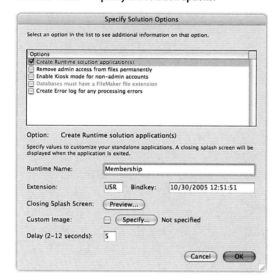

Final Thoughts

You can expand this project far beyond membership and dues to cover a variety of situations. Another extension is to publish it to the Web with Instant Web Publishing, which is demonstrated in the next project. All of the security features that you have created here are automatically transferred to the Web. Thus, you have an example of a project that can be run using FileMaker, using the runtime solution you have created here, and as a Web-based solution that people can access with a web browser.

CHAPTER 11: Implementing a Simple Web Publishing Solution

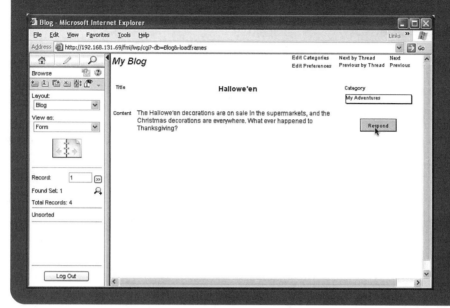

About the Project

Web sharing is the primary goal of this project. You can enter data into your database from a web browser; other people can view the data using web browsers. Somewhere, FileMaker needs to be running with a network connection so people can connect to the database, but that is the only needed copy of FileMaker.

Each entry into the blog can be linked to others. In this project, a response to a blog posting is itself a blog posting, not a comment. Self-joins and a link field link each blog posting.

Prerequisites

This project relies on the Shell.fp7 table for setting up its tables. You also need a network connection in order to connect to the database.

@work resources

Please visit the publisher's website to access the following Chapter 11 files:

▶ **Blog.fp7**

▶ **Shell.fp7**

Planning the Project

This project implements a generic blog that enables you to post items to your blog easily. Each item may have a category associated with it, and the project provides basic navigation tools.

If you are implementing a web-based publishing solution for a specific purpose, you might have additional fields that are relevant to your particular line of work.

You can test the database on your own computer, but network access requires a network connection. It also requires that your firewall be configured to allow access on port 80 (the default port on which a web server runs). If you are running on a commercial Internet service provider, you can run FileMaker and Instant Web Publishing on your local area network; however, in order to allow access from the outside, you need your ISP to assign you a static IP address or reserve a specific DHCP address for you. And you also might need to upgrade to a business account that allows you to run a web server.

Finally, there are limits to the number of clients that can be hosted with FileMaker Pro 8 and FileMaker Server 8. Check the FileMaker website for the current limits for the products to see where your project fits in.

Project: Blog

We'll be creating the Blog solution in 10 easy steps:

STEPS ▼

1. Getting started
2. Creating the Categories value list
3. Preparing the Blog layout
4. Setting Instant Web Publishing privileges in the database
5. Turning on Instant Web Publishing and sharing the database
6. Using a browser to connect to the blog
7. Implementing a Respond button
8. Creating the relationships
9. Cleaning up the layouts
10. Implementing navigation

STEP 1 ▼
Getting Started

Create the Blog database with the Blog table in it. Add or import the five administrative fields used in each project in this book. Add four fields to the blog table:

- ▶ Title (text)
- ▶ Content (text)
- ▶ Category (number)
- ▶ Link (number)

Figure 11.1 shows the table.

Add a second table, `Categories`, as shown in Figure 11.2. This table has the name and number for each category. The `Category ID` field should be an auto-enter serial number.

Finally, create the `Preferences` table. This table contains information that refers to the entire blog. For now, it needs only one field, `gBlogTitle`. As the name implies, it is a global. As you add other preferences to this table they, too, will probably be globals because they apply to the entire blog and every record within it.

If you look at the Relationships tab of the Define Database dialog, your database should look like Figure 11.3. There are no relationships drawn yet, but the three tables should be visible.

FIGURE 11.1 **Create the** `Blog` **table.**

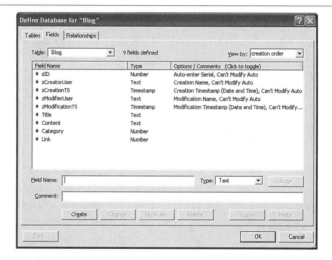

FIGURE 11.2 **Create the** `Categories` **table.**

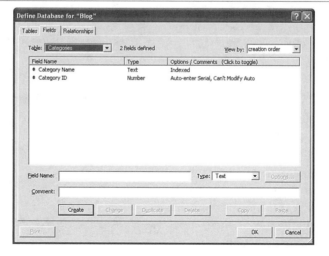

FIGURE 11.3   The three
tables of the database are
created.

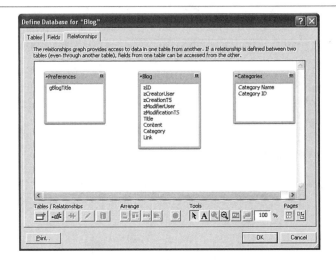

STEP 2 ▼
Creating the Categories Value List

Each blog entry has a numeric category. This value is not initialized, which means that each blog posting starts out not being categorized. A drop-down menu in the interface allows users to select a category for each posting. You can't change a categorized posting back to an uncategorized posting, although you are able to change it to another category.

You have already created the Categories table, so, even though there is no data in it yet, you can build a value list on the values that will exist in a field of that table. The trick here is to use the new feature of FileMaker Pro 8 that allows you to store a numeric value while displaying a more-understandable text value in the value list. (The feature is actually more general than that—you could store a text value and

display a numeric value—but this is the most common use of it.)

From the File menu, choose Define Value Lists and, in the dialog that opens, choose the first radio button (Use Values from Field) and then specify the field. The field on which you want to base the value list is the Category ID field, which is the number. This is shown in Figure 11.4.

FIGURE 11.4   Create the Categories value list.

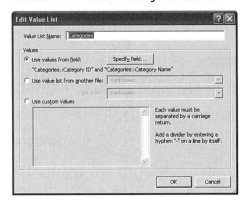

When you specify the field, the dialog shown in Figure 11.5 opens. On the left, make certain that you choose Category ID. On the right, use the check box at the top to indicate that you also want to display data from another field (Category Name). The Display Options in the lower right enable you to choose to display only the second field, the category name, in the list. Rest assured, however, that the value you are choosing is the category ID.

FIGURE 11.5   Specify the fields for the value list.

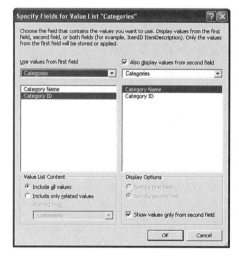

STEP 3 ▼
Preparing the Blog Layout

As usual, FileMaker is building default layouts for you. Go to the Blog layout and clean it up a bit so it can serve as the basis for the layout you will use on the Web.

In the header, place the Preferences::gBlogTitle field as a merge field. Set its font size and style to large and bold (or whatever suits you).

In the body of the layout, format that Title and Content fields as you see fit. The Link and Category fields can be removed for now. The layout should look like Figure 11.6 (subject to changes that you might make for aesthetic reasons).

FIGURE 11.6 **Prepare the basic Blog layout.**

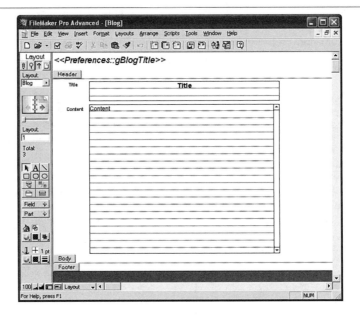

STEP 4 ▼
Setting Instant Web Publishing Privileges in the Database

You need to enable Instant Web Publishing in the database for the privilege set(s) that

will need it. When you choose Define Accounts & Privileges in the File menu, the dialog normally opens with a view onto accounts as shown in Figure 11.7.

Choose the Privilege Sets tab as shown in Figure 11.8.

FIGURE 11.7 **Define Accounts & Privileges opens on the Accounts tab.**

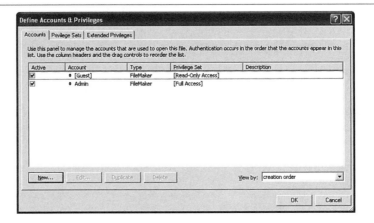

FIGURE 11.8 Select a privilege set to edit.

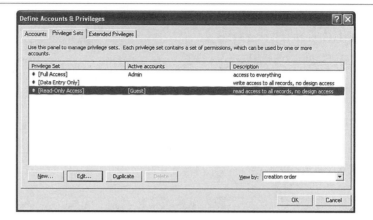

You need to edit each privilege set that will be used by Instant Web Publishing users. When you choose to edit a privilege set, the dialog shown in Figure 11.9 opens. Note that the privilege sets in square brackets are defined by FileMaker and cannot be modified in most cases; however, the Instant Web Publishing setting is modifiable (as are all the networking settings).

In the Extended Privileges section at the lower left, make certain that access via Instant Web Publishing is turned on.

NOTE

The two default accounts ([Guest] and Admin) use the default [Read-Only Access] and [Full Access] privilege sets. They are sufficient for the Blog example, but you might want to add another privilege set and one or more accounts that use it. This privilege set would allow updating records (that is, adding blog entries and responding to them) while not allowing full access. Preventing guests from updating the blog itself is not unusual.

FIGURE 11.9 Edit the privilege set.

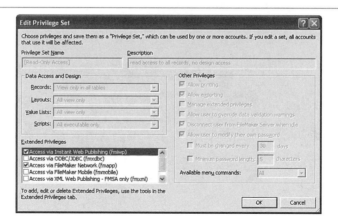

STEP 5 ▼
Turning on Instant Web Publishing and Sharing the Database

In the Blog layout, choose Instant Web Publishing from the Sharing submenu. This is one of the few cases in which the interface for Windows differs from that of Mac OS X.

In Windows, as shown in Figure 11.10, the Sharing submenu is in the Edit menu; in Mac OS X, it is in the FileMaker Pro application menu. The functionality is the same in both operating systems after you have chosen Instant Web Publishing.

If Instant Web Publishing is not on, turn it on with the radio button at the top of the dialog shown in Figure 11.11.

FIGURE 11.10 Choose Instant Web Publishing from the Sharing submenu.

FIGURE 11.11 Set up Instant Web Publishing.

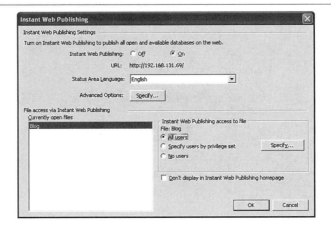

FileMaker displays the URL of the computer on which you are running. This might take a while to appear, so do not worry if there is a delay. If FileMaker cannot turn on Instant Web Publishing, you receive an error message. The Electronic Documentation folder that is located inside the FileMaker folder contains details on Instant Web Publishing. If you get an error, check in the documentation to see what it means. Fortunately, in most cases, Instant Web Publishing just works. (If it doesn't, it might be because you have already configured a web server to run on your computer, and you need to change the default port number as described in the documentation.)

After Instant Web Publishing is turned on, check that the Status Area language is what you want it to be. Select the database in the lower left and choose the type of access you want to allow. If the database does not appear in the list at the lower left, check to make certain that it is open.

Before closing this window, write down the URL; you need it to connect to the Instant Web Publishing database. Of course, you can also copy the URL and paste it into your browser.

STEP 6 ▼
Using a Browser to Connect to the Blog

Launch your browser, and type or paste the URL into the address field. Figure 11.12 shows the browser opening to the FileMaker home page.

You type in the URL provided when setting up Instant Web Publishing, and as soon as your browser tries to connect, it is redirected to the home page. In Figure 11.12, the URL typed in was http://192.168.131.69; the address shown in the browser's address window was generated automatically as it connected to the home page.

FIGURE 11.12 The database should appear on the Instant Web Publishing home page.

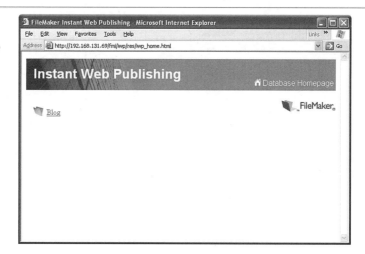

If the database does not appear, go back to the Instant Web Publishing setup and make certain that the check box in the lower right that controls whether it is listed on the home page is checked. Also, recheck the Extended Privileges to make certain that the database supports Instant Web Publishing access.

When you select the database, you are prompted to log in, as shown in Figure 11.13.

You now access the database. The layout you have created is very basic, but it should appear as shown in Figure 11.14.

FIGURE 11.13 **Log in to the database.**

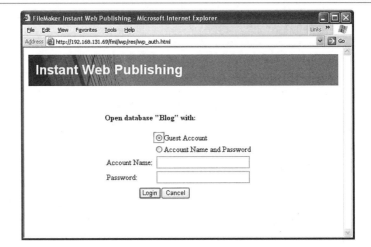

FIGURE 11.14 **The database is opened.**

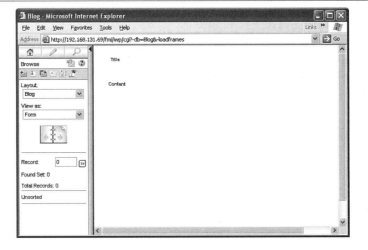

STEP 7 ▼
Implementing a Respond Button

The database has been set up with a Link field in the Blogs table to allow you to link one blog entry to another. Now it is time to implement that. There are two parts: You implement the script and button to respond to a blog posting by creating a new, linked posting, and then you need to implement relationships to move from one blog to another. In this step, you implement the script and the button.

This is similar to what you have done many times before now. Create a script that will be attached to a button. The script accepts a script parameter that is the ID of the original posting; it is used to set the Link field in the new posting, providing a link back.

The script is shown in Figure 11.15.

Create a button and attach the script to it. Remember to set the script parameter to the Blog::zID field.

STEP 8 ▼
Creating the Relationships

Two self-joins are needed to implement the links. Begin by creating two new tables in the Define Database dialog's Relationships tab. Both new tables should be based on Blog; name one Previous Blog and the other Response Blog.

Create a relationship from Link in Blog to zID in Previous Blog; create a relationship from zID in Blog to Link in Response Blog. The structure is shown in Figure 11.16.

FIGURE 11.15   Create a script to create a linked blog entry.

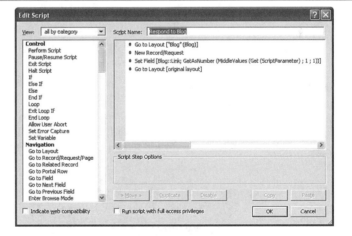

FIGURE 11.16   Create the
relationships.

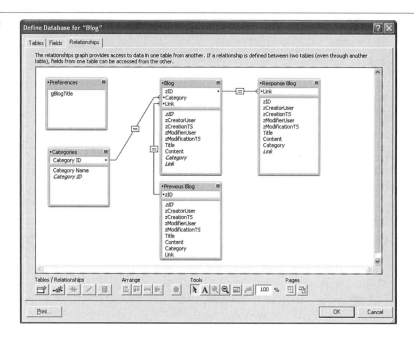

STEP 9 ▼
Cleaning up the Layouts

FileMaker has been creating default layouts for you as you have created tables. The Preferences and Categories layouts are needed to allow people to enter the blog title and to add new categories. You might choose to use the default layouts. Alternatively, you can modify them. Or, you can create new layouts based on the templates in the New Layout/Report dialog.

Each one should have a button on it that enables you to return to the Blog layout. Figure 11.17 shows the Categories layout with this modification. This was created by building a new layout using New Layout/Report and choosing the Standard Form layout type with the Windows standard screen layout theme. The title was added along with the Return to Blog button that goes to the Blog layout. In this case, the default Categories layout was then deleted from the database file.

FIGURE 11.17   Add a
Return to Blog button to
Preferences and Categories.

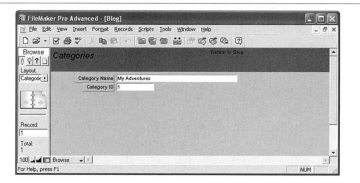

In the Blog layout, add a drop-down menu for the Category field.

STEP 10 ▼
Implementing Navigation

All of the pieces of the solution are now in place. Figure 11.17 shows what the finished Blog layout looks like in the solution.

Here is what you need to do to complete it.

In the header, add the six navigation fields shown at the right of the layout. Each is text that is selected and formatted as a button. Here is what the buttons do:

▶ **Edit Categories**—Go to the Categories layout

▶ **Edit Preferences**—Go to the Preferences layout

▶ **Next by Thread**—Go to Related Record from Response Blog using the Blog layout

▶ **Previous by Thread**—Go to Related Record from Previous Blog using the Blog layout

▶ **Next**—Go to Record [Next]

▶ **Previous**—Go to Record [Previous]

Test the solution in FileMaker, and then access it from a web browser. If the navigation buttons work in FileMaker itself, they should work properly in the web browser. The only detail that you might have to worry about is that sometimes different web browsers image text slightly differently. A good rule of thumb is to leave a little extra space around text so it is not accidentally cut off by the browser.

FIGURE 11.18 The finished Blog layout provides navigation.

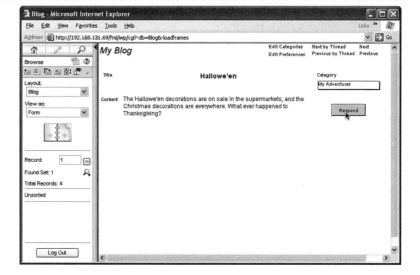

Final Thoughts

The steps to publish a database on the Web with Instant Web Publishing are so simple that, after you have done it once, you might never look back. The key to an effortless Instant Web Publishing deployment is to get things working properly locally when you access the database with FileMaker. Make certain that buttons and navigation tools are functioning properly; they should function properly on the Web.

Then, access the database with a variety of browsers running on a variety of operating systems. Look for cut-off text in fields that need enlarging. Check that security works.

The projects in this book have covered a variety of features of FileMaker Pro 8 in a number of contexts. Only one major item is left: How you get there from here. The final project deals with conversion of pre-FileMaker 7 database files.

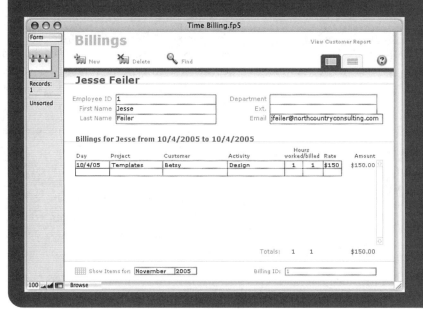

About the Project

This final project addresses the issues in converting to the new FileMaker Pro file and database structure intoduced in FileMaker Pro 7 and used today in FileMaker Pro 8. This conversion project is based on the FileMaker 6 Time Billing template. The Time Billing template is shown in the opening figure. In the center of the layout, a portal displays records from the Time Billing Line Items relationship.

Prerequisites

Learn about the database you are converting and about the features available in the latest version of FileMaker. View the old database in an native (older) verison of FileMaker if you can. Before you begin, make a copy of the old database files to work on while keeping a backup copy in a safe place.

@work resources

Please visit the publisher's website to access the following Chapter 12 files:

- ▶ Conversion.log
- ▶ Import.log
- ▶ Time Billing.fp7

Planning the Project

This project is not the same type of sequential project you have seen in other chapters. The first step in planning consists of the collection of information described in the previous section. Then, consider using the steps that follow in whatever sequence seems to address whatever problems you uncover.

The beginning in most cases consists of opening the database in FileMaker 7 or FileMaker 8; FileMaker will convert the database. The conversion is automatic, and it is done automatically for all versions of FileMaker. A conversion log reports on the process.

The automated conversion is designed to transform the old database and its data (or multiple databases and their data) to FileMaker 7. A conversion log is generated so you can see what has been done.

Restructuring the databases to take advantage of new features cannot be done automatically. For example, database files can now contain multiple tables. The automated conversion does not combine tables from several files; you wind up with database files with single tables, just as you had in the old version. You can then go on to combine them (as you will see in this project), but it is not done automatically.

Another issue in database conversion is that, by definition, you are dealing with old databases. They might be a few months old, or they might be years old. They might have been modified by many hands; or, even if they are your own, you might have learned over the years how to do things in better ways. As a result, you might have inconsistent data-naming conventions, a variety of scripts, and so forth. Automated conversion does not clean up any of this.

In an ideal world, the conversion process would start with a full understanding of the old database, proceed through a conversion process that builds on the automated conversion, and continue with a process that takes advantage of the new FileMaker features. In the real world, parts of this process are able to be achieved.

One important point to remember about using the new FileMaker features, such as multiple tables per file and script parameters, is that they frequently make the code that you have to write in calculations and scripts much simpler. There can be tremendous savings, but they come at the cost of manual conversion.

Finally, it is worth noting that some areas of conversion can be problematic. Many people have discovered that conversion problems seem to relate more to the way in which database solutions are structured than to the size and complexity of a project. Obviously, a large project might have more areas that could pose problems, but a well-written large project might have fewer problems than a poorly written small one. And it is not just poorly written solutions that might have problems. Well-written solutions that used features that are no longer available or that did not use features that are now available might incur difficulties.

This in no way means that you should not convert your databases. In fact, because the new features in FileMaker 7 databases are so powerful, the sooner you convert the better. What it does mean is that you should prepare for the issues that might arise. Search the FileMaker website for *conversion*. You will find a number of references that you can download, including an 80-page document, "Converting FileMaker Databases from Previous Versions," which is located at http://filemaker.com/downloads/pdf/fm8_converting.pdf.

Your range of tools is broad: You can try the built-in conversion and, many times, that will be the end of the matter because it will succeed. You can also prepare by reading documents such as the ones on the FileMaker website that should get you up to speed for a complex conversion. Or, resources such as this chapter can help you with a middle-ground conversion that has some common problems, but not a host of problems.

 TIP

You can take another route that might be very efficient. FileMaker is very good at importing and exporting data. You can build a new FileMaker solution that uses the new features, and then import the data from an old file. It might be easiest to open the old file in an old copy of FileMaker and export the data in tab-delimited format or one of the other transfer formats. Then, import it from the flat file. By setting out with new scripts and calculations but your old data intact, you might have the best of both old and new worlds.

Project: FileMaker Conversion

We'll be converting a database in nine easy steps:

STEPS ▼

1. Getting started
2. Reviewing field definitions
3. Reviewing value lists
4. Reviewing relationships
5. Running conversion
6. Reviewing converted field definitions and value lists
7. Reviewing converted relationships
8. Reviewing file references
9a. Consolidating tables (with FileMaker Pro Advanced)
9b. Consolidating tables (with other versions)

STEP 1 ▼
Getting Started

Back up the existing database safely. If you can, burn it to a CD or DVD and get the copy off your computer so there is no way you can accidentally touch the old files. As noted, review the documentation and output reports. Then get busy.

The first few steps require you to open the software in an old version of FileMaker. If you do not have it, you will have to skip these steps. Alternatively, you might find documentation from the old solution that provides this information. If you do, that is a help, but remember that there is no guarantee that documentation is up to date.

STEP 2 ▼
Reviewing Field Definitions

Start by looking at the field definitions. Those for Time Billing are shown in Figure 12.1.

You might want to print this dialog. You can print it with screen capture, FileMaker Developer, or in the print dialog's FileMaker options. There is no one answer to how to do this because it depends on which version of FileMaker you are running. If you have the old software, you can always re-open the Define Fields dialog whenever you need to look at it, so a printed copy is not necessary.

Before continuing, spot-check the field definitions for calculations that involve relationships. You might not have heard the last of them.

FIGURE 12.1 Review field definitions.

Remember to review field definitions for related files. In pre-FileMaker 7 solutions, related tables are in related files, so if your solution has several files, it probably has relationships. (Some solutions are in a single folder with multiple files in it, but there might be no relationships.)

The Time Billing Line Items field definitions are shown in Figure 12.2.

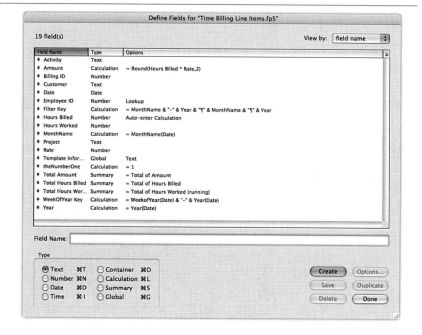

FIGURE 12.2   Review field definitions for related files.

STEP 3 ▼
Reviewing Value Lists

The value lists in Time Billing are shown in Figure 12.3.

Look for value lists with a source that is from a relationship. You will want to check these later.

STEP 4 ▼
Reviewing Relationships

Relationships might break during conversion or as a result of cleaning up file references later on. Make certain you know at least the general structure of the solution.

The relationships for Time Billing are shown in Figure 12.4.

FIGURE 12.3 **Review value lists.**

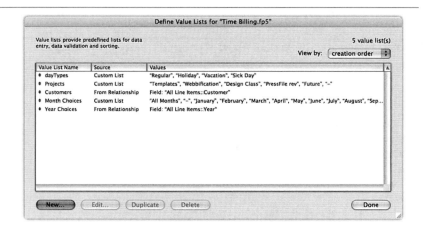

FIGURE 12.4 **Review** `Time Billing` **relationships.**

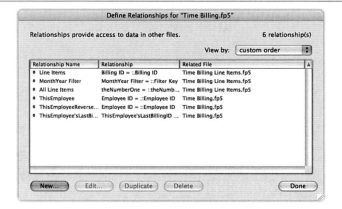

The new database model has relationships that are automatically bi-directional. That was not true in older versions of FileMaker. As a result, a relationship might need two declarations. The Time Billing relationship in the `Time Billing Line Items` file is shown in Figure 12.5. It is the reverse path of the Line Items relationship shown in the `Time Billing` file in Figure 12.4.

FIGURE 12.5 **Review** `Time Billing Line Items` **relationships.**

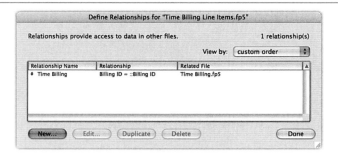

STEP 5 ▼
Running Conversion

For a single file, you can open it in FileMaker Pro 7 or FileMaker Pro 8. For a set of files to be converted, select them and drag them to the FileMaker Pro icon to open them all at once. You see the dialog shown in Figure 12.6.

FIGURE 12.6   Choose the conversion options for files.

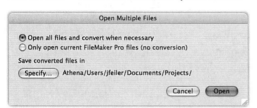

Choose the Open All Files and Convert When Necessary option. Also, it is a very good idea to specify a location for the converted files—preferably a new folder. Then you will be certain that everything is safely out of the way.

Conversion might take a while. When it is complete, a log file is created as shown in Figure 12.7. Open it and scan through it. It might be very lengthy, so do not worry about reading every line. What you are looking for are errors. If the conversion process high-lights specific errors, they are worth reviewing.

FIGURE 12.7   Review the conversion log.

```
⊖ ⊖ ⊖                            Conversion.log
10/31/2005 2:44:15 PM, Time Billing Line Items.fp7, 0, Conversion started.
10/31/2005 2:44:15 PM, Time Billing Line Items.fp7, 0, Version: Pro 5.0 - 6.0.
10/31/2005 2:44:15 PM, Time Billing Line Items.fp7, 0, 5 file references were converted.
10/31/2005 2:44:15 PM, Time Billing Line Items.fp7, 0, 1 relationships were converted.
10/31/2005 2:44:15 PM, Time Billing Line Items.fp7, 0, 9 calculations were converted.
10/31/2005 2:44:15 PM, Time Billing Line Items.fp7, 0, 0 container objects were converted.
10/31/2005 2:44:15 PM, Time Billing Line Items.fp7, 0, 0 layout images were converted.
10/31/2005 2:44:15 PM, Time Billing Line Items.fp7, 0, 19 fields were converted.
10/31/2005 2:44:15 PM, Time Billing Line Items.fp7, 0, 0 records were converted.
10/31/2005 2:44:15 PM, Time Billing Line Items.fp7, 0, 0 indexes recreated.
10/31/2005 2:44:15 PM, Time Billing Line Items.fp7, 0, 2 access privileges were converted.
10/31/2005 2:44:15 PM, Time Billing Line Items.fp7, 0, 0 value lists were converted.
10/31/2005 2:44:15 PM, Time Billing Line Items.fp7, 0, 4 layouts were converted.
10/31/2005 2:44:16 PM, Time Billing Line Items.fp7, 0, Verify Windows Print Setup settings: Customer Report.
10/31/2005 2:44:16 PM, Time Billing Line Items.fp7, 0, 9 scripts were converted.
10/31/2005 2:44:16 PM, Time Billing Line Items.fp7, 0, Deleting unneeded file reference: TimeBillingLineItems.
10/31/2005 2:44:16 PM, Time Billing Line Items.fp7, 0, Deleting unneeded file reference: Time Billing Line Items.
10/31/2005 2:44:16 PM, Time Billing Line Items.fp7, 0, Deleting unneeded file reference: Time Billing 2.
10/31/2005 2:44:16 PM, Time Billing Line Items.fp7, 0, Conversion completed.
10/31/2005 2:44:16 PM, Time Billing.fp7, 0, Conversion started.
10/31/2005 2:44:16 PM, Time Billing.fp7, 0, Version: Pro 5.0 - 6.0.
10/31/2005 2:44:16 PM, Time Billing.fp7, 0, 4 file references were converted.
10/31/2005 2:44:16 PM, Time Billing.fp7, 0, 6 relationships were converted.
10/31/2005 2:44:16 PM, Time Billing.fp7, 0, 15 calculations were converted.
10/31/2005 2:44:17 PM, Time Billing.fp7, 0, 2 container objects were converted.
10/31/2005 2:44:17 PM, Time Billing.fp7, 0, 6 layout images were converted.
10/31/2005 2:44:17 PM, Time Billing.fp7, 0, 30 fields were converted.
10/31/2005 2:44:17 PM, Time Billing.fp7, 0, 0 records were converted.
10/31/2005 2:44:17 PM, Time Billing.fp7, 0, 0 indexes recreated.
10/31/2005 2:44:17 PM, Time Billing.fp7, 0, 2 access privileges were converted.
10/31/2005 2:44:17 PM, Time Billing.fp7, 0, 5 value lists were converted.
10/31/2005 2:44:17 PM, Time Billing.fp7, 0, 6 layouts were converted.
10/31/2005 2:44:17 PM, Time Billing.fp7, 0, 30 scripts were converted.
10/31/2005 2:44:17 PM, Time Billing.fp7, 0, Deleting unneeded file reference: Time Billing Line Items 2.
10/31/2005 2:44:17 PM, Time Billing.fp7, 0, Conversion completed.
```

STEP 6 ▼
Reviewing Converted Field Definitions and Value Lists

A quick review of these is sufficient at this point. What you are looking for is references to related fields in calculations that might have broken in the conversion process. Chances are that all is well.

Sometimes a calculation is not converted properly, and FileMaker leaves the partially converted calculation in the database for you to fix. If you see a Field reference to <Field Missing>, you need to correct the problem. In a more extreme case, FileMaker might comment out a section of a script or calculation. If you can open the previous version of the database with an older version of FileMaker, you can see what the original code was and reconstruct it in the converted file.

STEP 7 ▼
Reviewing Converted Relationships

Although the structure of relationships is very different, most converted relationships seem to be fine at this point.

STEP 8 ▼
Reviewing File References

This step often uncovers problems and even causes new ones. Start by making a backup copy of the database.

Look at the file references using the Define File References command in the File menu. You should see something like the file references shown in Figure 12.8.

FIGURE 12.8   Review file references.

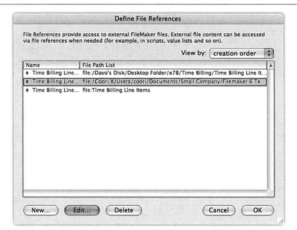

Before FileMaker Pro 7, file references weren't explicitly visible. As a result, many older FileMaker files have references that are deliberately or accidentally outdated.

In Figure 12.8, the first two file references point to specific disks that were probably used in testing. If you double-click a single file reference, you see the file path list for that reference, as shown in Figure 12.9.

FileMaker looks for each of the locations specified in the file path in order to find the file that satisfies the file reference. In this case, the file that satisfies the reference will most likely be Time Billing because most people do not have a disk with the name of the first path.

Remove paths that you do not have, but make certain to leave one or more paths that you do have. For most people, the path to the file by name is valid, particularly if that file is located in the same folder with the other database file.

Also check that paths are valid. A known culprit is blanks at the end of file names.

When you have cleaned up file references, check that you have not broken relationships or references to related fields in calculations.

📌 TIP

In tracking down errors in converted solutions, file references are a good place to start. One of the symptoms of a problem with a file reference is an error that appears sometimes and not at other times. Because file references are resolved when FileMaker needs to get to a file, it is possible for files to be opened (and file references used) in a different sequence depending on what you do. Maddening errors that come and go apparently at random might well be file reference errors.

FIGURE 12.9 Examine file paths.

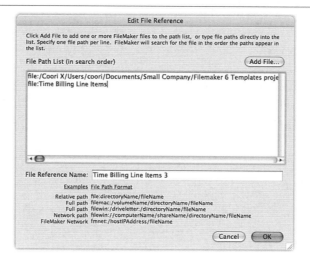

STEP 9A ▼
Consolidating Tables (with FileMaker Pro Advanced)

With many solutions, you might want to consolidate tables from several files. You cannot easily do this if those separate files are used in relationships from several other files, but in the case of a structure such as `Time Billing` and `Time Billing Line Items`, it is probably a good idea to consolidate them.

Begin by opening the Tables tab in the Define Database dialog of `Time Billing` (or whatever your main file is). Click Import in the lower right, and locate the related file. You are presented with a dialog to choose which table to import: This is easy because in pre-FileMaker 7 days there was only one table per file.

After the import, a dialog presents a summary of what has happened, as shown in Figure 12.10.

If there are any errors, open the log, as shown in Figure 12.11.

The relationship graph might already have a table with the name of the table you are importing, so the imported table has been renamed.

FIGURE 12.10   Review table import summary.

Go into the relationship graph and rename the first table, as shown in Figure 12.12.

Having disposed of the first table with that name, you can now rename the new table (`Table Billing Line Items 2`, in this case) as `Table Billing Line Items`.

Now, change the relationship to point to the imported table rather than the table in the external file.

First, check to see what the relationship is (by clicking the box in the middle of the line related to the two tables). Then, double-click the top of each table for a related file (the table name is in italics), and change the specification to the table in the current file as shown in Figure 12.13. When you close that dialog, the table name is in normal type, not italics.

FIGURE 12.11   Review the log.

```
11/1/2005 3:29:01 PM, Time Billing.fp7, 0, Import operations started
11/1/2005 3:29:20 PM, Time Billing.fp7, 0, Import of tables from file "Time Billing Line Items.fp7" started
11/1/2005 3:29:20 PM, Time Billing.fp7, 0, Table "Time Billing Line Items" imported as "Time Billing Line Items 2"
since a table or table occurrence named "Time Billing Line Items" already exists.
11/1/2005 3:29:20 PM, Time Billing Line Items 2::Billing ID, 1204, Field referred to in the calculation "Left(‹Field
Missing›; Position(‹Field Missing›; "-"; 1; 1) -1 )" is missing.
11/1/2005 3:29:20 PM, Time Billing Line Items 2::Employee ID, 1204, Field referred to in the calculation "Right
(‹Field Missing›; Length(‹Field Missing›) - Position(‹Field Missing›; "-"; 1;1) )" is missing.
11/1/2005 3:29:20 PM, Time Billing Line Items 2, 0, fields imported : 19
11/1/2005 3:29:20 PM, Time Billing.fp7, 0, tables imported : 1
11/1/2005 3:29:20 PM, Time Billing.fp7, 0, Import completed
```

FIGURE 12.12 Switch the names of the old and imported table.

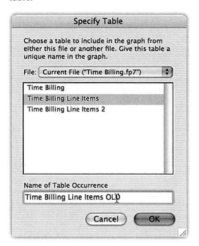

FIGURE 12.12 Switch the names of the old and imported table.

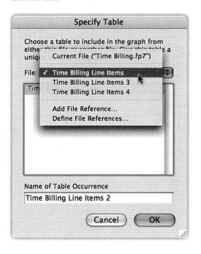

FIGURE 12.13 Change tables to point to tables in the current file.

Check that the relationship is correct; if not, change it.

When you have finished, all of the tables are in your file. Once again, review calculations and value lists to make certain that they have not been broken.

STEP 9B ▼
Consolidating Tables (with Other Versions)

The process is the same as consolidating tables with FileMaker Pro Advanced, but the sequence is different.

Start by renaming the table representing the external file (`Billing Line Items`, in this example). Call it something such as `Billing Line Items OLD`.

Then create a new table in the Tables tab; call it by the rightful name (such as `Billing Line Items`). Create the fields in that table manually.

Then, in the relationship graph, change the tables to point to the table in the current file and check that the relationships are correct as shown in Figure 12.14. The point to note here is that the table names are not italicized: They are located in this database file now.

Once again, review calculations and value lists to make certain that they have not been broken.

FIGURE 12.14 The
finished relationship graph.

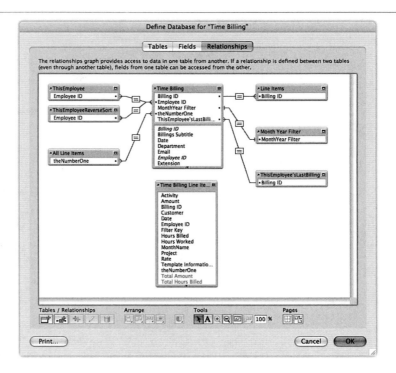

Final Thoughts

Converting FileMaker solutions is an
acquired skill. It is often a matter of trial and
error because the things that can go wrong
are so often dependent on what someone (or
many people) did in designing and modifying the old database long, long ago.

PART III: Appendixes

Error Code	Description
-1	Unknown error.
0	No error.
1	User canceled action.
2	Memory error.
3	Command is unavailable (for example, wrong operating system, wrong mode, and so forth).
4	Command is unknown.
5	Command is invalid (for example, a Set Field script step does not have a calculation specified).
6	File is read-only.
7	Running out of memory.
8	Empty result.
9	Insufficient privileges.
10	Requested data is missing.
11	Name is not valid.
12	Name already exists.
13	File or object is in use.
14	Out of range.
15	Can't divide by zero.
16	Operation failed, request retry (for example, a user query).
17	Attempt to convert foreign character set to UTF-16 failed.
18	Client must provide account information to proceed.
19	String contains characters other than A–Z, a–z, 0–9 (ASCII).
100	File is missing.
101	Record is missing.
102	Field is missing.
103	Relationship is missing.
104	Script is missing.
105	Layout is missing.
106	Table is missing.

Error Code	Description
107	Index is missing.
108	Value list is missing.
109	Privilege set is missing.
110	Related tables are missing.
111	Field repetition is invalid.
112	Window is missing.
113	Function is missing.
114	File reference is missing.
115	Specified menu set is not present.
130	Files are damaged or missing and must be re-installed.
131	Language pack files are missing (such as template files).
200	Record access is denied.
201	Field cannot be modified.
202	Field access is denied.
203	No records in file to print, or password doesn't allow print access.
204	No access to field(s) in sort order.
205	User does not have access privileges to create new records; import will overwrite existing data.
206	User does not have password change privileges, or file is not modifiable.
207	User does not have sufficient privileges to change database schema, or file is not modifiable.
208	Password does not contain enough characters.
209	New password must be different from existing one.
210	User account is inactive.
211	Password has expired.
212	Invalid user account and/or password. Please try again.
213	User account and/or password does not exist.
214	Too many login attempts.

Error Code	Description
215	Administrator privileges cannot be duplicated.
216	Guest account cannot be duplicated.
217	User does not have sufficient privileges to modify administrator account.
300	File is locked or in use.
301	Record is in use by another user.
302	Table is in use by another user.
303	Database schema is in use by another user.
304	Layout is in use by another user.
306	Record modification ID does not match.
400	Find criteria are empty.
401	No records match the request.
402	Selected field is not a match field for a lookup.
403	Exceeding maximum record limit for trial version of FileMaker Pro.
404	Sort order is invalid.
405	Number of records specified exceeds number of records that can be omitted.
406	Replace/Reserialize criteria are invalid.
407	One or both match fields are missing (invalid relationship).
408	Specified field has inappropriate data type for this operation.
409	Import order is invalid.
410	Export order is invalid.
412	Wrong version of FileMaker Pro used to recover file.
413	Specified field has inappropriate field type.
414	Layout cannot display the result.
415	One or more required related records are not available.
500	Date value does not meet validation entry options.
501	Time value does not meet validation entry options.
502	Number value does not meet validation entry options.

APPENDIX A   FileMaker Error Codes

Error Code	Description
503	Value in field is not within the range specified in validation entry options.
504	Value in field is not unique as required in validation entry options.
505	Value in field is not an existing value in the database file as required in validation entry options.
506	Value in field is not listed on the value list specified in validation entry option.
507	Value in field failed calculation test of validation entry option.
508	Invalid value entered in Find mode.
509	Field requires a valid value.
510	Related value is empty or unavailable.
511	Value in field exceeds maximum number of allowed characters.
600	Print error has occurred.
601	Combined header and footer exceed one page.
602	Body doesn't fit on a page for current column setup.
603	Print connection lost.
700	File is of the wrong file type for import.
706	EPSF file has no preview image.
707	Graphic translator cannot be found.
708	Can't import the file or need color monitor support to import file.
709	QuickTime movie import failed.
710	Unable to update QuickTime file reference because the database file is read-only.
711	Import translator cannot be found.
714	Password privileges do not allow the operation.
715	Specified Excel worksheet or named range is missing.
716	A SQL query using DELETE, INSERT, or UPDATE is not allowed for ODBC import.
717	There is not enough XML/XSL information to proceed with the import or export.

Error Code	Description
718	Error in parsing XML file (from Xerces).
719	Error in transforming XML using XSL (from Xalan).
720	Error when exporting; intended format does not support repeating fields.
721	Unknown error occurred in the parser or the transformer.
722	Cannot import data into a file that has no fields.
723	You do not have permission to add records to or modify records in the target table.
724	You do not have permission to add records to the target table.
725	You do not have permission to modify records in the target table.
726	There are more records in the import file than in the target table. Not all records were imported.
727	There are more records in the target table than in the import file. Not all records were updated.
729	Errors occurred during import. Records could not be imported.
730	Unsupported Excel version. (Convert file to Excel 7.0 (Excel 95), Excel 97, 2000, or XP format, and try again).
731	The file you are importing from contains no data.
732	This file cannot be inserted because it contains other files.
733	A table cannot be imported into itself.
734	This file type cannot be displayed as a picture.
735	This file type cannot be displayed as a picture. It will be inserted and displayed as a file.
736	Too much data to export to this format. It will be truncated.
800	Unable to create file on disk.
801	Unable to create temporary file on System disk.

Error Code	Description	Error Code	Description
802	Unable to open file.	922	User dictionary cannot be found.
803	File is single user or host cannot be found.	923	User dictionary is read-only.
804	File cannot be opened as read-only in its current state.	951	An unexpected error occurred (*).
		954	Unsupported XML grammar (*).
805	File is damaged; use `Recover` command.	955	No database name (*).
806	File cannot be opened with this version of FileMaker Pro.	956	Maximum number of database sessions exceeded (*).
807	File is not a FileMaker Pro file or is severely damaged.	957	Conflicting commands (*).
		958	Parameter missing (*).
808	Cannot open file because access privileges are damaged.	1200	Generic calculation error.
		1201	Too few parameters in the function.
809	Disk/volume is full.	1202	Too many parameters in the function.
810	Disk/volume is locked.	1203	Unexpected end of calculation.
811	Temporary file cannot be opened as FileMaker Pro file.	1204	Number, text constant, field name, or (expected.
813	Record Synchronization error on network.	1205	Comment is not terminated with `* /`.
814	File(s) cannot be opened because maximum number is open.	1206	Text constant must end with a quotation mark.
815	Couldn't open lookup file.	1207	Unbalanced parenthesis.
816	Unable to convert file.	1208	Operator missing, function not found, or (not expected.
817	Unable to open file because it does not belong to this solution.	1209	Name (such as field name or layout name) is missing.
819	Cannot save a local copy of a remote file.	1210	Plug-in function has already been registered.
820	File is in the process of being closed.	1211	List usage is not allowed in this function.
821	Host forced a disconnect.	1212	An operator (for example, +, –, *) is expected here.
822	FMI files not found; re-install missing files.	1213	This variable has already been defined in the `Let` function.
823	Cannot set file to single-user, guests are connected.	1214	AVERAGE, COUNT, EXTEND, GETREPETITION, MAX, MIN, NPV, STDEV, SUM, and GETSUMMARY: Expression found where a field alone is needed.
824	File is damaged or not a FileMaker file.		
900	General spelling engine error.		
901	Main spelling dictionary not installed.		
902	Could not launch the Help system.	1215	This parameter is an invalid `Get` function parameter.
903	Command cannot be used in a shared file.		
905	No active field selected; command can only be used if there is an active field.	1216	Only Summary fields allowed as first argument in GETSUMMARY.
920	Can't initialize the spelling engine.		
921	User dictionary cannot be loaded for editing.		

Error Code	Description
1217	Break field is invalid.
1218	Cannot evaluate the number.
1219	A field cannot be used in its own formula.
1220	Field type must be normal or calculated.
1221	Data type must be number, date, time, or timestamp.
1222	Calculation cannot be stored.
1223	The function is not implemented.
1224	The function is not defined.
1300	The specified name can't be used.
1400	ODBC driver initialization failed; make sure the ODBC drivers are properly installed.
1401	Failed to allocate environment (ODBC).
1402	Failed to free environment (ODBC).
1403	Failed to disconnect (ODBC).
1404	Failed to allocate connection (ODBC).
1405	Failed to free connection (ODBC).
1406	Failed check for SQL API (ODBC).
1407	Failed to allocate statement (ODBC).
1408	Extended error (ODBC).

* These are only for FileMaker databases published on the Web.

Here are some URLs that can provide additional information about FileMaker. Note that they are useful in their own right, but they also can contain links to further resources.

This Book's Resources

Sams Publishing. The publisher's website contains information about the book and ordering information. Even more important, the files to download for this book are available there. Search for ISBN 0672328569. www.samspublishing.com.

Philmont Software Mill. The author's website includes information about FileMaker (and other products) as well as copies of the files for this book and a Q&A section. www.philmontmill.com.

FileMaker Resources

FileMaker Online Help. Search for error codes, functions, and script steps to find the complete lists and documentation for each one.

FileMaker website. Use this site for information about FileMaker products, support, downloads, and links to further information. www.filemaker.com.

FileMaker Solutions Alliance. Sponsored by FileMaker, this group provides additional support for a nominal fee. An annual conference provides essential information about FileMaker. www.filemaker.com/developers/join_fsa.html.

FileMaker Advisor. This magazine provides ongoing news and information for advanced developers. http://filemakeradvisor.com/.

Relational Databases

National Academies Press. Chapter 6, "The Rise of Relational Databases," in *Funding a Revolution*. www.nap.edu/readingroom/ books/far/ch6.html. This is a fairly detailed description of the history of relational databases. It is of more than passing interest because the capabilities of today's databases were very much determined by the events of the 1970s that are recounted here.

Security

National Institute of Standards and Technology. Search on *database* or *database security* to find the latest and most definitive guides to high-level security. www.nist.gov/.

Graphics and Interface

Edward Tufte is the definitive author of books and articles on the visual presentation of information. www.edwardtufte.com/tufte/.

account   An account with name and password assigned to an individual or group of individuals. The account's access is defined by the privilege set with which it is associated.

AND   The Boolean operator that is true only if both conditions are met.

breakpoint   An indication that processing of a script should stop before a certain step. At that point, you can choose to continue with the script, examine data, or step through the steps. Breakpoints are used in debugging.

Browse mode   The FileMaker mode in which you enter and look at data.

cardinality   The number of elements possible on each side of a relationship (one-to-many, one-to-one, and many-to-many). Note that in most cases zero is a possible value for each side.

custom menu   A specific menu with its commands that you create or modify.

custom menu set   A set of custom menus that you can attach to a given layout.

data viewer   A tool in FileMaker Advanced that enables you to examine and change the values of data as a script is executing. The data viewer assists in debugging.

drop-down calendar   A new interface element that makes date entry easy for users.

equijoin A relationship between two tables that relies on equality between two fields (Account ID = Customer ID, for example).

factor Separating interface elements and operations from the fundamental operations of the solution. Well-factored solutions are amenable to scripting and easy conversion to the Web because their original interfaces are not entangled with the desktop.

Find mode The FileMaker mode in which you search for data.

firewall Hardware and/or software that blocks messages except to specific ports. For FileMaker, ports 80, 591, and 5003 might need to be opened.

global field This is a field that contains a single value for the database table; each record can access this single value. Often global fields were used in pre-FileMaker 7 solutions to handle tasks that can be handled with script parameters or with variables.

join table An intermediate table used to implement a many-to-many relationship. The join table itself might never be seen.

Layout mode The mode for creating layouts and reports. Enter Layout mode by choosing Layout mode from the View menu or clicking the Layout icon (the T-square) at the top of the status area.

many-to-many relationship A relationship with many elements on both sides. For example, classes-to-students can be many-to-many. One student may take many classes, and one class may have many students.

merge field Fields that are displayed on a layout as text, not editable fields. They are useful for titles. However, remember that because they are not fields, they can never be used for data entry. You might be better off using fields that do not allow data entry in Browse mode but do allow data entry in Find mode. Merge fields behave like word processing objects, however, sliding together as necessary.

normalization A set of structured processes to organize relational database information in the simplest manner.

one-to-many relationship A relationship in which one side has only one element. One warehouse may contain many inventory items.

one-to-one relationship A relationship with only one element on each side. Often this type of relationship is used for optimizing data storage or enforcing security.

one-to-table and many-to-table relationships Relationships in which a field in one table is related to a global field with a single value in another table so that all records in the first table relate to a single record in the second table.

OR The Boolean operator that is true if either condition is met.

port A subdivision of an IP address that is used for routing specific types of messages. A web server (which is what FileMaker Instant Web Publishing is) runs on port 80 in most cases and requests for web pages are sent there. If you are already running a web server, you need to use an alternate port for FileMaker; port 591 has been reserved for this purpose. For FileMaker Server, port 5003 also needs to be opened.

portal A scrolling list displaying records from a relationship. Depending on settings, you can sort rows in a portal, enter new records, modify records, and even delete records.

Preview mode   The FileMaker mode that displays data as it will be printed. Buttons and other interface elements are not usable because they are not usable on printed output.

privilege set   A collection of privileges specifying access to records, layouts, and menus. Privilege sets are generally shared by a number of accounts. Privilege sets include extended privileges that enable you to control access through networking and the Web. In addition, privilege sets can be used to control exporting and printing of data.

relational database   A database (such as FileMaker) in which data is stored in one or more tables. These can be related to one another using common fields.

relationship graph   The diagram shown in the Relationships tab of the Design Database dialog. It shows tables, fields, and relationships.

runtime solution   A standalone FileMaker solution that allows access to a non-networked database; runtime solutions do not support networking.

schema   The structure of a database.

self-join   A relationship from one table to itself. It is implemented by creating an alias to the table and joining the two tables in the relationship graph as if they were different tables.

status area   The area at the left of FileMaker windows that contains controls. It can be shown or hidden. The tools and controls in the status area change depending on the current mode.

tab control   A new feature in FileMaker 8 that allows you to draw a section of tabs in a layout. When displayed in FileMaker 7, the tabs are all visible, layered on top of one another.

unique identifier   When items in the database need to be uniquely identified, it is generally best to give them a meaningless number (such as an auto-entered serial number generated by FileMaker). Avoid creating identifiers that combine meaningful information (location, vendor, and so forth). When an identifier has no meaning, an object's attributes (stored in other fields) can change without destroying the identifier.

validation   Rules that you set in the Validation tab of the Options dialog. They determine if a field must be entered, must be unique, and so forth. You can control the implementation of these rules by allowing users to override them. In general, preventing any overrides means that your database data will be as clean as possible. (To implement validation rules that sometimes apply, it might be best to implement them with scripts or calculations.)

value list   A list of values to be displayed in a drop-down menu or other interface element. A value list can also be used to specify a custom sort order. Value lists can contain specific values that you type in; they also can contain values from fields. They might consist of pairs of values: One value is used for the data, and a second value from a record is used as the displayed item in the value list (FileMaker Pro 8 only).

variable   In FileMaker Pro 8, a variable can be declared in a script. It can store data used throughout the script; its name begins with $. A global variable is available to any script after it has been declared; its name begins with $$.

Index

Symbols

Numbers

A

account privileges
  Idea Tracker database, 122-125
  setting, 122-125

accounts
  creating, 124
  membership list, 168
  privileges
    Idea Tracker database, 122-125
    setting, 122-125

Address field (Students table), 138

addresses (IP), static, 125

aliases, 88-89

ampersand (&), 124

and operator, 14, 124

architecture (scripts)
  atomic and self-contained scripts, 27
  comments, 26
  factoring, 27-28
  readability and reuse, 26-27

atomic scripts, 27

Auto-Enter tab (Options dialog), 59

auto-entries, 59

automation, 23
  calculations, 36
  runtime (standalone) solutions, 37-38
  scripts, 24-26
    atomic and self-contained scripts, 27
    comments, 26
    committing and reverting records, 32
    conditional (If) script steps, 31
    cutting and pasting script steps, 30
    Data Viewer, 34-35
    debugging, 32-34

disabling script steps, 29-30
editing, 24
factoring, 27-28
loop (Repeat) script steps, 31-32
parameters, 35-36
readability and reuse, 26-27
reordering script steps, 25
Set Error Capture, 28-29
variables, 32
writing, 24-26

B

Blog table, 174-175

blogs
  Blog table, 174-175
  Categories table, 175
  Categories value lists, 176-177
  connecting to, 181-182
  Instant Web Publishing
    privileges, 178-179
    turning on, 180-181
  layout
    cleaning up, 184-185
    creating, 177
  navigation, 185
  planning, 174
  Preferences table, 175
  prerequisites, 173
  relationships, 183
  Respond buttons, creating, 183

Boutique Manager project
  completed layout, 96
  data entry, enabling, 92-94
  default Categories layout, 95

J-K-L

Q-R

Run button (Script Debugger), 33

runtime solutions, 37-38, 169-170

S

Sams Publishing website, 207

scope of projects, 42

Script Debugger, 33-34

script steps

  conditional (If), 31

  cutting and pasting, 30

  disabling, 29-30

  loop (Repeat), 31-32

  reordering, 25

ScriptMaker, 24. *See also* scripts

ScriptMaker button (Script Debugger), 34

scripts

  atomic and self-contained scripts, 27

  attaching to buttons, 94

  Class Enrollment project, 142

  comments, 26

  Data Viewer, 34-35

  debugging, 32-34

  editing, 24

  factoring, 27-28

  Idea Tracker database, 121

  New Dues, 163-164

  parameters, 35-36

  Project Management database, 109-111

  readability and reuse, 26-27

  records

    committing and reverting, 32

    creating, 135-136

script steps

  conditional (If), 31

  cutting and pasting, 30

  disabling, 29-30

  loop (Repeat), 31-32

  reordering, 25

  Set Error Capture, 28-29

  variables, 32

  writing, 24-26

searching databases, 13-15

security

  account privileges, 122-125

  firewalls, 127, 174

  membership list, 168-169

  National Institute of Standards and
  Technology, 208

  planning, 44

self-join relationships, 100, 104

servers

  FileMaker Server, 50

  web server, 130

Set Error Capture (scripts), 28-29

Set Next Step button (Script Debugger), 34

Set/Clear Breakpoint button (Script Debugger), 34

sharing databases

  FileMaker Server, 50

  FileMaker sharing, 49-50

  web sharing, 50

Sharing menu commands, Instant Web Publishing, 180

solutions. *See* projects

Sort Records command (File menu), 15

sorting data, 15-16

Specify Calculation dialog, 123

spreadsheets, 10, 50-51

standalone (runtime) solutions, 37-38, 169-170

troubleshooting

    error codes, 201-205

    scripts

        Data Viewer, 34-35

        debugging, 32-34

        Set Error Capture, 28-29

Tufte, Edward, 208

turning on Instant Web Publishing, 180-181

U-V

unneeded data, eliminating, 51

validation rules, 60

value lists

    Categories value lists (blogs), 176-177

    creating, 80-81

    reviewing, 191, 194

variables, 32

Vendor ID field (Inventory database), 54

versions of FileMaker, 8-9

View menu commands, Find Mode, 13

views

    Form, 17

    list view, 17

    table view, 17

W

web publishing. *See* Instant Web Publishing

web servers, 130

web sharing, 50

websites

    Edward Tufte, 208

    FileMaker, 207

    FileMaker Advisor, 207

    FileMaker Online Help, 207

    FileMaker Solutions Alliance, 207

    National Institute of Standards and Technology, 208

    Philmont Software Mill, 207

    Sams Publishing, 207

writing scripts, 24-26

    atomic and self-contained scripts, 27

    comments, 26

    factoring, 27-28

    readability and reuse, 26-27

X-Y-Z

zCreationTS field (Inventory database), 55

zCreator field (Inventory database), 55

zID field (Inventory database), 54

zModificationTS field (Inventory database), 55

zModifier field (Inventory database), 55